Building Background Knowledge for Academic Subjects

Fundamental Reading

Michael A. Putlack
Stephen Poirier
Tony Covello

PLUS 2

DARAKWON

Fundamental Reading PLUS 2

Publisher Chung Kyudo
Authors Michael A. Putlack, Stephen Poirier, Tony Covello
Editors Jeong Yeonsoon, Zong Ziin, Kim Namyeon
Designers Park Narae, Elim

First published in January 2020
By Darakwon, Inc.
Darakwon Bldg., 211, Munbal-ro, Paju-si, Gyeonggi-do 10881
Republic of Korea
Tel: 82-2-736-2031 (Ext. 250)
Fax: 82-2-732-2037

ISBN 978-89-277-0860-5 54740
      978-89-277-0856-8 54740 (set)

www.darakwon.co.kr

Photo Credits
Federico Rostagno (p. 10), Igor Plotnikov (p. 19), studiolaska (p. 55), Barry
Paterson (p. 68), Hans Christiansson (p. 97), My Good Images (p. 101), 1000
Words (p. 103) / www.shutterstock.com
Collier's, illustration by Frederic Remington (p. 96), File:Collier's-Remington-3
-18-05.jpg / https://commons.wikimedia.org/wiki/

Components Main Book / Workbook
11 10 9 8 7 6 5   23 24 25 26 27

Fundamental Reading

PLUS 2

DARAKWON

How to Use This Book

This book has 8 chapters that cover different academic subjects. Each chapter is composed of 2 units based on interesting topics related to the subject.

Student Book

Think about the Topic
Two warm-up questions are provided to motivate students to think about the topic before continuing with the unit.

Vocabulary Preview
Students can learn the key words from the passage and get ready to read.

Background Knowledge
Students can read brief information that will help them predict and understand the main reading passage.

Main Reading Passage
The passages discuss topics that have been carefully chosen to provide academic knowledge as well as to interest students. Each passage is between 290–320 words long.

QR code for listening to the passage

Finding the topic of each paragraph

Finding the main topic or main idea of the passage

Additional information and further learning about the topic

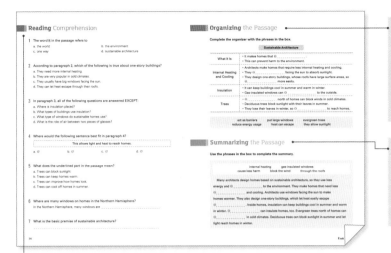

Organizing the Passage

By completing a graphic organizer or a Fill in a Table question, students can review and recognize important ideas and information presented in the passage.

Summarizing the Passage

By completing a regular summary or a Prose Summary question, students can review the main points of the passage once again.

Reading Comprehension

5 multiple-choice questions and 2 short-answer questions are given to help students master various types of questions.

TOEFL Practice Test

At the end of the book, there is a supplementary TOEFL Practice Test section containing four passages. Each passage has six questions similar to ones that frequently appear on real TOEFL tests.

Workbook

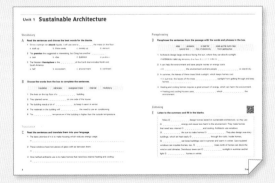

The first part contains 4 types of exercises, which provide students with a deeper understanding of the passage as well as enhanced vocabulary and language skills.

The second part presents a writing topic related to the reading passage. Students can develop their thoughts on the topic, conduct further research on their own, and learn to write a short paragraph.

Table of Contents

Chapter **1**
Architecture

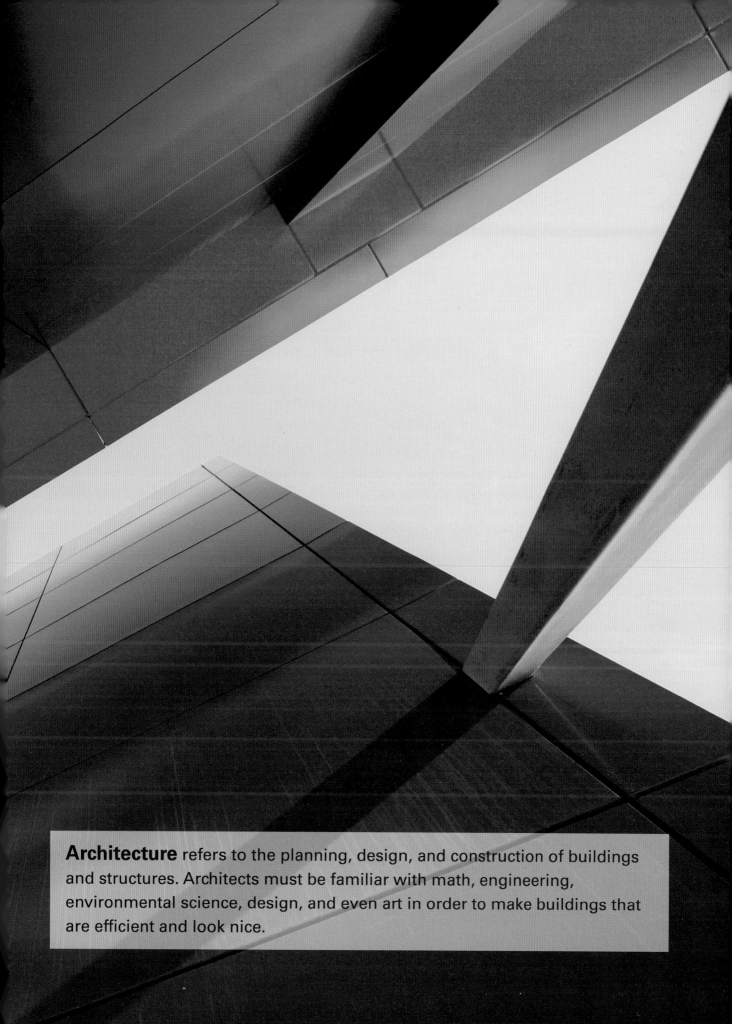

Architecture refers to the planning, design, and construction of buildings and structures. Architects must be familiar with math, engineering, environmental science, design, and even art in order to make buildings that are efficient and look nice.

Unit 1

Sustainable Architecture

Think about the Topic

1 What should architects consider when designing buildings?

2 What are some ways that architects can help the environment?

Vocabulary Preview

A **Match the words with their definitions by writing the correct letters in the blanks.**

1 sustainable   _____   a. a half of the Earth

2 premise   _____   b. to get rid of; to end

3 internal   _____   c. to take in; to soak up

4 absorb   _____   d. having two or more floors

5 hemisphere   _____   e. able to be kept going or reused

6 surface area   _____   f. in or on the inside of something

7 multistory   _____   g. an idea that supports an argument

8 insulation   _____   h. a tree that keeps its leaves all year long

9 evergreen tree   _____   i. the total area of the outside of an object

10 eliminate   _____   j. material that prevents or reduces the passing of heat or cold air

B **Choose the words that have similar** (*sim.*) **or opposite** (*opp.*) **meanings from the box.**

obstacle	build	external

1 construct   _____ *sim.*

2 internal   _____ *opp.*

3 barrier   _____ *sim.*

Background Knowledge

Nowadays, architects are focusing on creating efficient buildings. These ecofriendly buildings can reduce the amount of materials used to make them. They can also help buildings use less electricity by making them more efficient. This sustainable architecture is becoming more popular each year.

Sustainable Architecture

Q

What is each paragraph mainly about?

P1 What sustainable architecture is and (when / why) people are focusing on it

P2 How architects make homes which need (less / more) internal heating and cooling

P3 How _____ can help keep buildings cool and warm

Around the world, people are focusing on the environment. One way they can take care of it is to construct homes based on **sustainable** architecture. The basic **premise** of it is to make housing which reduces energy usage. Heating and cooling homes requires a great amount of
5 energy, which can harm the environment.

One method architects use is to make homes that need less **internal** heating and cooling. Homes in cold climates must be heated. So architects design large windows facing the sun, where they can **absorb** sunlight. The sunlight increases homes' internal temperatures. In the Northern
10 **Hemisphere**, many windows are on the southern sides of homes. As for houses in hot climates, they need less internal heat. So architects make buildings that let heat escape. They often design one-story buildings. These have roofs with greater **surface areas** in comparison to **multistory** homes. Thus
15 heat can more easily escape through the roofs.

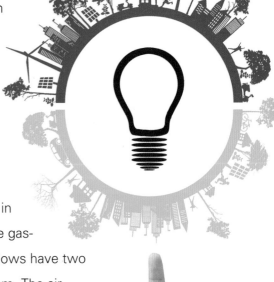

Inside homes, architects rely on **insulation**. This is material placed inside walls. It makes
20 internal temperatures different from outside ones. It can therefore keep buildings cool in summer and warm in winter. Sustainable homes often use gas-insulated windows, too. These windows have two
25 pieces of glass with air between them. The air acts as a barrier to the outside. This gives it an insulating effect.

Outside homes, <u>trees can act as blankets for homes</u>. In cold climates, northern winds can hit buildings with freezing temperatures. Thus architects place **evergreen trees** north of homes to block the wind. ❶ *Deciduous trees are better for locations south of homes. ❷ In summer, the leaves of these trees block sunlight, which keeps homes cool. ❸ During winter, their leaves have fallen off. ❹

Sustainable architecture uses many factors to reduce energy usage. This **eliminates** the need for excessive heating and cooling. So it can help the environment and save people money on energy costs.   Words 317

*deciduous tree: any type of tree that loses its leaves in winter

P4 How architects can use _____ when designing homes

i According to one study, buildings use almost half of all the energy consumed on the Earth. They also consume about twenty-five percent of all drinking water and create about twenty percent of all solid waste. Reducing these numbers is one goal of sustainable architecture.

 Check the main idea of the passage.

  a. Heating and cooling are important for all types of buildings.

  b. Multistory buildings are more difficult to build than one-story ones.

  c. There are many ways to use sustainable architecture in buildings.

  d. Architects must use efficient materials when designing buildings.

Reading Comprehension

1 The word it in the passage refers to

   a. the world

   b. the environment

   c. one way

   d. sustainable architecture

2 According to paragraph 2, which of the following is true about one-story buildings?

   a. They need more internal heating.

   b. They are very popular in cold climates.

   c. They usually have big windows facing the sun.

   d. They can let heat escape through their roofs.

3 In paragraph 3, all of the following questions are answered EXCEPT:

   a. Where is insulation placed?

   b. What types of buildings use insulation?

   c. What type of windows do sustainable homes use?

   d. What is the role of air between two pieces of glasses?

4 Where would the following sentence best fit in paragraph 4?

This allows light and heat to reach homes.

   a. ❶   b. ❷   c. ❸   d. ❹

5 What does the underlined part in the passage mean?

   a. Trees can block sunlight.

   b. Trees can keep homes warm.

   c. Trees can improve how homes look.

   d. Trees can cool off homes in summer.

6 Where are many windows on homes in the Northern Hemisphere?

In the Northern Hemisphere, many windows are _____.

7 What is the basic premise of sustainable architecture?

_____

Organizing the Passage

Complete the organizer with the phrases in the box.

	Sustainable Architecture
What It Is	• It makes homes that ❶_____. • This can prevent harm to the environment.
Internal Heating and Cooling	• Architects make homes that require less internal heating and cooling. • They ❷_____ facing the sun to absorb sunlight. • They design one-story buildings, whose roofs have large surface areas, so ❸_____ more easily.
Insulation	• It can keep buildings cool in summer and warm in winter. • Gas-insulated windows can ❹_____ to the outside.
Trees	• ❺_____ north of homes can block winds in cold climates. • Deciduous trees block sunlight with their leaves in summer. • They lose their leaves in winter, so ❻_____ to reach homes.

act as barriers	put large windows	evergreen trees
reduce energy usage	heat can escape	they allow sunlight

Summarizing the Passage

Use the phrases in the box to complete the summary.

internal heating	gas-insulated windows
cause less harm	block the wind through the roofs

Many architects design homes based on sustainable architecture, so they use less energy and ❶_____ to the environment. They make homes that need less ❷_____ and cooling. Architects use windows facing the sun to make homes warmer. They also design one-story buildings, which let heat easily escape ❸_____. Inside homes, insulation can keep buildings cool in summer and warm in winter. ❹_____ can insulate homes, too. Evergreen trees north of homes can ❺_____ in cold climates. Deciduous trees can block sunlight in summer and let light reach homes in winter.

Unit 2
Shipping Container Homes

Think about the Topic

1 What are shipping containers normally used for?

2 What do you think a shipping container home is like?

Vocabulary Preview

A **Match the words with their definitions by writing the correct letters in the blanks.**

1 schooling _____ a. to change

2 secure (v.) _____ b. a small area of land

3 freighter _____ c. to give up; to leave

4 withstand _____ d. to obtain; to get a hold of

5 transform _____ e. already having been made

6 premade _____ f. to resist; to stand up against

7 compact _____ g. a ship used to transport goods

8 plot _____ h. arranged in a fairly small space

9 ecofriendly _____ i. education a person receives at school

10 abandon _____ j. helping or not harmful to the environment

B **Choose the words that have similar (*sim.*) or opposite (*opp.*) meanings from the box.**

separate	strong	rural

1 tough _____ *sim.*

2 urban _____ *opp.*

3 combine _____ *opp.*

Background Knowledge

Young people often have trouble finding cheap housing. This is especially true in large cities, where rent and housing prices are high. As a result, many young people choose to have roommates to share housing costs. Others who wish to live alone are finding different ways to acquire cheap housing. Some of these ways are quite unique.

Shipping Container Homes

Q

What is each paragraph mainly about?

P1 The reason young people search for (cheap / convenient) housing

P2 How _____ shipping containers are

P3 The price _____ of shipping container homes

P4 The benefits of shipping container homes being (compact / large)

In recent years, housing prices in urban areas have risen greatly. After young people complete their **schooling**, they often cannot **secure** well-paying jobs. They therefore search for _____ housing that is cheap. One of the most unique is the shipping container home.

5 Shipping containers are used to move goods on **freighters** across the oceans. These containers are very tough. They can **withstand** winds blowing more than 100 miles per hour, and giant waves more than fifty feet high will not hurt them either. Their only real weakness is that they are made of steel so can rust.

10 A standard shipping container measures forty feet long by eight feet wide by eight feet high. Young people today are **transforming** these metal boxes into homes. They have numerous advantages. One is that they are much cheaper than regular homes. **Premade** homes can be purchased online for around $12,000. That is much less than the hundreds of thousands—or

15 even millions—of dollars that homes sell for in some urban areas.

Since many young people are single, they require little space. The **compact** sizes of shipping container homes therefore make them ideal places to reside in. The homes are also mobile since they can be transported on the backs of

20 trucks. In some urban areas, landowners rent tiny **plots** of land for people to put their homes on.

▲ Container apartments for students in France © Igor Plotnikov

For those individuals who want bigger spaces, two or more shipping containers can be combined. This gives people more living space while still keeping costs down. Some architects have made creative designs by arranging multiple containers into unique shapes. An added advantage is that these homes are **ecofriendly**. Each year, 500,000 containers are **abandoned**. So people living in these homes are recycling several tons of steel.

While these homes are not for everyone, they are making housing in urban areas cheap and convenient. That is making them popular with the younger generation. Words 317

P5 How shipping container homes can be (comfortable / creative) and helpful to the environment

i In the United States, New York, Los Angeles, and San Francisco are some of the most expensive places to live. Chicago, Boston, and Washington, D.C. are also expensive. Shipping container homes can be found in or near all of these large urban centers.

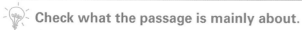
Check what the passage is mainly about.

   a. How many people live in shipping container homes

   b. The places where shipping container homes are common

   c. The benefits of living in a shipping container home

   d. The types of designs used for shipping container homes

Reading Comprehension

1   What is the best choice for the blank?

   a. large   b. alternative   c. distant   d. common

2   The word them in the passage refers to

   a. goods on freighters

   b. these containers

   c. giant waves

   d. winds blowing more than 100 miles per hour

3   According to the passage, which of the following is true about shipping container homes?

   a. They can only be put in certain areas.

   b. They are cheaper than other houses in urban areas.

   c. They cannot provide enough space for a family to live in.

   d. They are not strong enough to replace regular houses.

4   The word mobile in the passage is closest in meaning to

   a. inexpensive   b. portable   c. safe   d. convenient

5   In paragraph 5, all of the following questions are answered EXCEPT:

   a. How can people make their shipping container homes larger?

   b. How can shipping container homes benefit the environment?

   c. What do some architects do with shipping container home designs?

   d. What are some of the unique shapes some shipping container homes have?

6   Why do many young people require little space?

Many young people require little space since _____.

7   What is a weakness of shipping containers?

_____

Organizing the Passage

Complete the organizer with the phrases in the box.

Shipping Container Homes

Shipping Containers	• They are used to move ❶_____. • They are tough and can withstand strong winds and giant waves. • They measure forty feet long by ❷_____ by eight feet high.
Advantages of Shipping Container Homes	• Premade shipping container homes can be bought online ❸_____. • They are compact, so they are ideal places for single young people. • ❹_____ and can be moved around on the backs of trucks. • Two or more of them ❺_____ to give people more space. • By living in a shipping container home, a person is recycling ❻_____.

can be combined	goods on freighters	for around $12,000
several tons of steel	eight feet wide	they are mobile

Summarizing the Passage

The first sentence of a short summary is provided below. Complete the summary by choosing THREE answer choices that express the most important ideas.

There are several advantages to living in a shipping container home.

1 It is possible to purchase a shipping container home for a cheaper price than a regular house.

2 Shipping containers are very strong and can be moved from place to place.

3 Young people are starting to find alternative housing like shipping container homes in big cities.

4 Not everyone is interested in living in shipping container homes despite them being convenient.

5 Shipping container homes are not only compact but are also good for the environment.

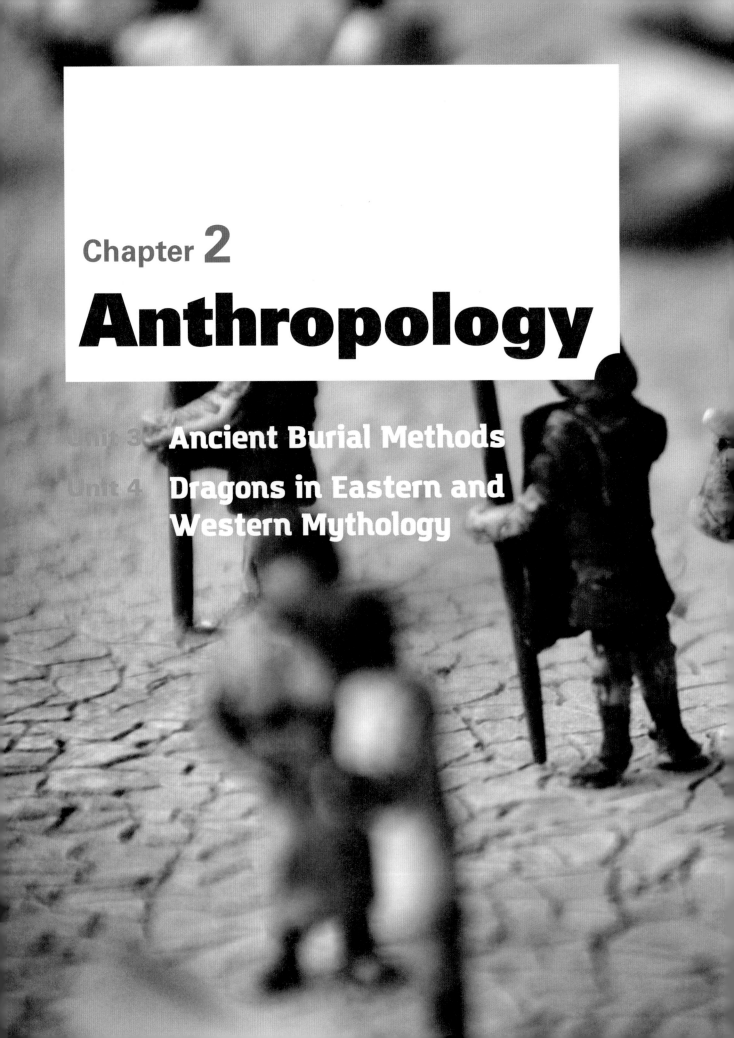

Chapter 2
Anthropology

Anthropology refers to the study of human societies and how humans behaved in the past. Anthropologists study human cultures and civilizations and try to learn how humans acted in the past and why they acted in particular ways.

Unit 3
Ancient Burial Methods

Think about the Topic

1 Why do you think people bury the dead?

2 In your country, do people bury the dead or do something else with their bodies?

Vocabulary Preview

A Match the words with their definitions by writing the correct letters in the blanks.

1 prehistoric _____   a. dead; no longer living

2 deceased _____   b. the dead body of a person

3 hominid _____   c. in one piece; not damaged

4 rite _____   d. a place where the dead are buried

5 underworld _____   e. relating to the period before written history

6 remains _____   f. the place where the souls of the dead go

7 date (v.) _____   g. to determine how old someone or something is

8 mummy _____   h. a special ceremony held for religious or special reasons

9 cemetery _____   i. a dead body preserved by a special process used in
                                    ancient Egypt

10 intact _____   j. a member of the group containing all extinct and living
                                    humans and primates

B Choose the words that have similar (sim.) or opposite (opp.) meanings from the box.

grave	rarely	dead

1 departed _____ sim.

2 tomb _____ sim.

3 commonly _____ opp.

Background Knowledge

When people die, the living must do something with dead bodies.
Bodies left alone will decompose, and that will create bad smells
and could cause people to get sick. In addition, animals often eat
the remains of dead people. As a result, humans began taking care
of the dead, typically by burning the bodies or by burying them.

Ancient Burial Methods

Q

What is each paragraph mainly about?

P1 Why people began to (burn / bury) the dead

P2 How belief in the _____ led ancient people to bury the dead

P3 What archaeologists found in a (cave / funeral rite) in Israel

P4 What the ancient _____ did with their dead

Since **prehistoric** times, humans have buried people when they die. Some speculate that this began as a way to protect the dead from being eaten by animals. It may have also been a way to honor a **deceased** individual. Eventually, burying people took on a religious meaning in many
5 cultures around the world.

Both Neanderthals—**hominids** related to humans—and early modern humans buried their dead. Ancient people also held funeral **rites** for the deceased. Some think they may have buried their dead in the ground to send them to the afterlife more easily. After all, many cultures
10 considered the **underworld** to be where the souls of the departed went.

The oldest evidence of human burial comes from a cave in Israel. The **remains** have been **dated** to 100,000 B.C. In the cave were twenty-seven sets of remains. Archaeologists also found various items painted with red *ochre, which was often used in ancient funeral rites. People in ancient
15 cultures often buried their dead with objects from the deceased's life. Thus the items collected were likely important to the people they were found with.

In ancient Egypt, most people were buried in the ground. Their bodies
20 were well preserved thanks to the dry climate in the Egyptian desert. As for people in the upper class, they were buried in tombs. Yet deceased bodies did not preserve well in tombs above
25 ground. So the Egyptians began making **mummies** to preserve people's bodies.

▲ An ancient Egyptian mummy

▲ An ancient Roman cemetery located outside a city

During the republic years, the Romans burned their dead and placed the ashes in *urns. These urns were then buried either in the ground or in stone tombs. The dead were commonly buried together in **cemeteries** located outside cities and towns. During the time of the Roman Empire, burying bodies became more common. This was due to the _____ of Christianity in the empire. It called for people to be buried **intact**. Words 312

30

▲ Urn

*ochre: dirt mixed with iron that is often used to make colored paints
*urn: a vase in which the ashes of a burned body are kept

📃 How the (Romans / Christians) took care of their dead during the republic and empire years

ⓘ The Roman Republic lasted from 509 B.C. to 27 B.C. During this time, the Roman Senate, a group of elected leaders, ran Rome. The Roman Empire started with Emperor Augustus in 27 B.C. It lasted until 476 A.D. During this time, emperors ruled over Rome.

Check the main point of the passage.

a. Burning bodies was common in ancient cultures.

b. Only Egyptians made mummies of dead people.

c. Archaeologists are still learning about ancient burial methods.

d. People in ancient cultures often buried their dead in various ways.

Reading Comprehension

1 The word speculate in the passage is closest in meaning to

   a. know   b. write   c. guess   d. question

2 Why does the author mention Neanderthals?

   a. To argue that they often burned dead bodies

   b. To state that they buried people who died

   c. To claim that they were afraid of the afterlife

   d. To point out their relationship to modern humans

3 According to paragraph 3, which of the following is NOT true about the cave?

   a. It is located in Israel.

   b. Human remains were found there.

   c. People made items there to bury them with the dead.

   d. Archaeologists found items related to burial rites in it.

4 In paragraph 4, which of the following is mentioned about burial methods in ancient Egypt?

   a. How difficult it was to make mummies

   b. Which people were buried in pyramids

   c. Where people in the upper class were buried

   d. What kinds of items were buried along with the dead

5 What is the best choice for the blank?

   a. rise   b. threat   c. study   d. defeat

6 What happened to people buried in the ground in ancient Egypt?

   Their bodies were _____ .

7 What did the Romans do with the dead during the republic years?

   _____

Organizing the Passage

Complete the organizer with the phrases in the box.

Ancient Burial Methods	
Reasons to Bury the Dead	• Some people speculate the dead were buried to ❶_____ from eating them or to honor them. • The dead may have been buried to send them to the afterlife more easily.
Israel	• Remains of buried people dating to 100,000 B.C. were found ❷_____ in Israel. • Items used in funeral rites were found buried with the dead.
Egypt	• Many people were buried in the ground since ❸_____ preserved their bodies. • Members of ❹_____ were buried in tombs. • The Egyptians made mummies in order to preserve deceased bodies.
Rome	• The Romans burned bodies and ❺_____ in urns in the ground or in tombs during the republic years. • During the empire years, they buried bodies due to ❻_____.

the desert climate	buried the ashes	keep animals
the rise of Christianity	in a cave	the upper class

Summarizing the Passage

Use the phrases in the box to complete the summary.

preserve people's bodies		get to the afterlife
the ashes in urns	prehistoric times	have been dated

Humans have been burying the dead ever since ❶_____. They might have buried the dead to make it easier for them to ❷_____ in the underworld. The oldest buried human remains were found in a cave in Israel. The remains ❸_____ to 100,000 B.C. The ancient Egyptians buried people in the ground and also made mummies to ❹_____. During the Roman Republic, the Romans burned their dead and put ❺_____. During the Roman Empire, however, they buried people due to the influence of Christianity.

Unit 4

Dragons in Eastern and Western Mythology

Vocabulary Preview

A **Match the words with their definitions by writing the correct letters in the blanks.**

1 fearsome _____ a. a snake

2 feat _____ b. huge; very large

3 mythology _____ c. very frightening or scary

4 serpent _____ d. a great or important action

5 antler _____ e. to fall, often from a great height

6 gigantic _____ f. a horn with branches, like on a deer

7 plunge _____ g. the legends and stories of a group of people

8 worship _____ h. to honor or respect someone like a god by praying

9 kidnap _____ i. anything valuable, especially gold, silver, and jewels

10 treasure _____ j. to take a person somewhere against his or her will

B **Choose the words that have similar** (*sim.*) **or opposite** (*opp.*) **meanings from the box.**

possess	differ	dry

1 lack (*v.*) _____ *opp.*

2 watery _____ *opp.*

3 vary _____ *sim.*

Background Knowledge

Dragons are mythological creatures that appear in the stories of many cultures. There are tales of dragons in places such as Europe, India, China, and America. Nobody knows exactly when stories of dragons first started. But both the ancient Greeks and Sumerians told tales about them thousands of years ago.

Dragons in Eastern and Western Mythology

Most people can recognize a dragon instantly. It is a powerful, **fearsome** creature with a large body, a long neck, and a huge head. A dragon is a magical animal capable of various **feats**. It features in the **mythologies** of Eastern and Western cultures, yet the dragon is not the same in these
5 places.

Q

What is each paragraph mainly about?

P2 How dragons appear in (Eastern / Western) cultures

In Eastern cultures—particularly in China—the dragon resembles a **serpent**. Despite lacking wings, it can fly. A Chinese dragon has body parts similar to those of other animals. For instance, it may have **antlers** like a deer and claws like an eagle. It usually has scales like a fish, which is
10 unsurprising since Eastern dragons are associated with rain and water and live at the bottoms of lakes and oceans or high in the clouds.

P3 How dragons look in Western cultures and what can (kill / help) them

_____, Western dragons have larger bodies and resemble **gigantic** lizards. They have long wings, which allows them to fly. Unlike Eastern dragons, they can breathe fire, so they avoid watery places, which
15 can kill them. For instance, in the work *The Hobbit* by J.R.R. Tolkien, the dragon Smaug is killed after being struck by an arrow and then **plunging** into a deep lake.

P4 How people in Eastern cultures

_____

dragons

How people regard dragons also differs. In Eastern cultures, dragons are important mythical creatures and are believed
20 to be lucky. They can control the weather and cause rain to fall. Because many Eastern cultures relied upon agriculture, this caused people to **worship** dragons.

P5 Why people in Western cultures

_____

dragons

In Western cultures, dragons were not
25 worshiped but feared. They were evil creatures

▲ *Saint George and the Dragon*

▲ The Eastern dragon

that attacked castles and **kidnapped** people, especially princesses, to eat. They made *lairs in caves filled with **treasure** they had stolen. Knights in Western cultures often tried to kill dragons. *Saint George and the Dragon* is one story about the killing of a dragon that had kidnapped a princess.

Dragons around the world share some characteristics. Nevertheless, their ³⁰ appearances and actions vary in Eastern and Western cultures. **Words 317**

*lair: a place in the ground or in a cave where an animal lives

i Saint George is one of the most famous saints in Christianity. According to legend, he traveled to a foreign land and learned about a dragon that was killing people. Before it could kill a princess, he killed the dragon and freed the land from the monster.

 Check the main point of the passage.

a. People in different cultures had different views of dragons.

b. Dragons featured in stories where they were evil creatures.

c. Some dragons looked like serpents while others did not.

d. There are many stories about dragons that are told nowadays.

Reading Comprehension

1 According to the passage, how are Eastern dragons different from Western dragons?

   a. They look like big lizards.

   b. They do not have wings.

   c. They can breathe fire.

   d. They cannot fly.

2 The phrase associated with in the passage is closest in meaning to

   a. scared of   b. reported on   c. studied about   d. connected to

3 What is best choice for the blank?

   a. In contrast   b. Therefore   c. In other words   d. As a result

4 In paragraph 4, which of the following can be inferred about dragons in Eastern cultures?

   a. They lived in dry places.

   b. They had lots of treasure.

   c. Most people were afraid of them.

   d. Farmers in Eastern cultures liked them.

5 According to paragraph 5, which of the following is NOT true about dragons in Western cultures?

   a. They were able to be killed by people.

   b. They often attacked and killed people.

   c. They were worshiped by some people.

   d. They lived in caves that had treasure in them.

6 Where do Eastern dragons live?

Eastern dragons live _____.

7 How is the dragon Smaug killed?

_____

Organizing the Passage

Select the appropriate statements from the answer choices and match them to the dragon to which they relate. Two of the answer choices will NOT be used.

Eastern Dragon	Western Dragon
•	•
•	•
•	

1 Had body parts that resembled those of other animals

2 Preferred to live in a castle with its treasure

3 Was attacked by knights who were trying to kill it

4 Was considered a lucky animal and was worshiped

5 Could sometimes be the ruler of a land

6 Was able to control the weather

7 Could both fly and breathe fire

Summarizing the Passage

Use the phrases in the box to complete the summary.

can breathe fire   to be lucky
stories about knights   look like serpents   magical creatures

Dragons are ❶_____ that appear in the mythologies of Eastern and Western cultures. In Eastern cultures such as China, dragons ❷_____. They have the body parts of other animals and live in lakes and oceans or high in clouds. Western dragons look like gigantic lizards and ❸_____. In Eastern cultures, dragons are considered ❹_____, and they can control the weather and make rain fall. In Western cultures, dragons are feared because they are evil creatures. There are ❺_____ who try to kill dragons.

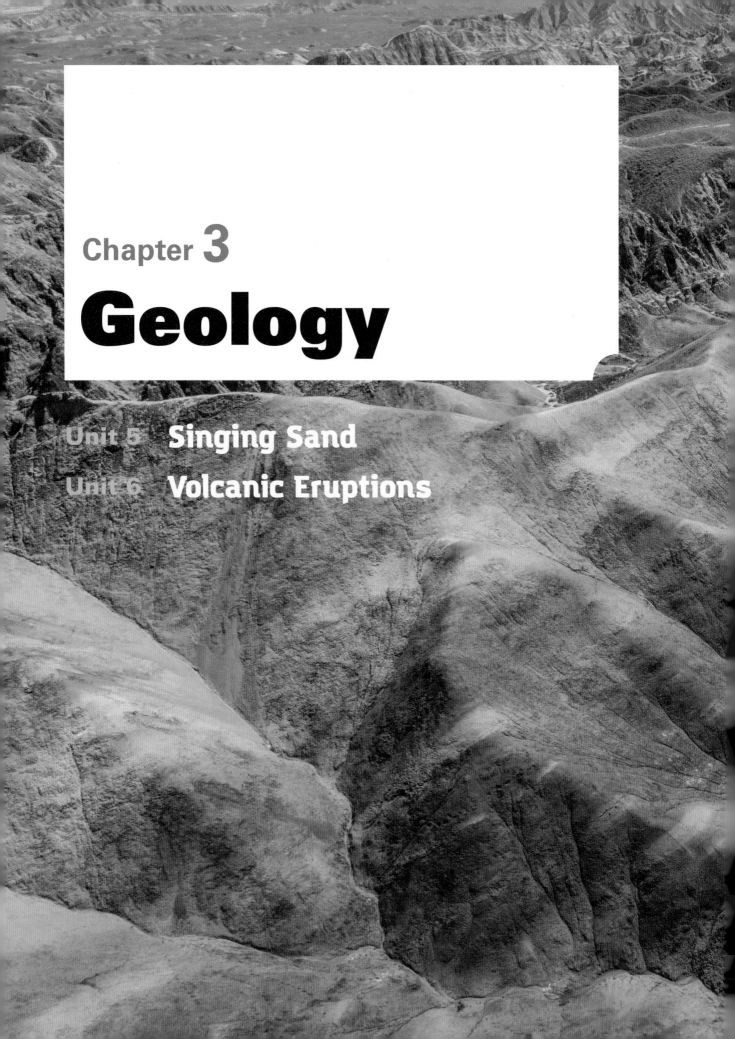

Chapter 3
Geology

Geology refers to the study of the earth and the rocks, minerals, and other things in it. Geologists study the features of the planet and try to learn what causes the planet to change and to undergo events such as volcanic eruptions and earthquakes.

Unit 5

Singing Sand

Think about the Topic

1 Where are the places on the Earth that sand is the most common?

2 What do you think singing sand is?

Vocabulary Preview

A **Match the words with their definitions by writing the correct letters in the blanks.**

1 rumble _____   a. to fall down

2 dune _____   b. to run into; to hit

3 phenomenon _____   c. exactly the same

4 accumulate _____   d. able to be heard

5 avalanche _____   e. a fact or event that is seen

6 tumble _____   f. to build up; to increase gradually

7 pitch _____   g. to make a low, deep sound like thunder

8 identical _____   h. the degree of height or depth of sound

9 collide _____   i. a sandy hill on a beach and or in a desert that is caused by the wind

10 audible _____   j. the sudden movement of snow, ice, dirt, etc. from a high place to a lower one

B **Choose the words that have similar** (*sim.*) **or opposite** (*opp.*) **meanings from the box.**

conceal	scared	investigation

1 frightened _____ *sim.*

2 research _____ *sim.*

3 reveal _____ *opp.*

Background Knowledge

Many deserts on the Earth contain huge amounts of sand. People assume that these deserts always look the same, but that is not true. When the wind blows, it causes the appearance of the desert to change. Blowing wind creates sand dunes of various heights as grains of sand pile up on top of one another.

Singing Sand

Q

What is each paragraph mainly about?

P1 How people felt about the noises they heard coming from (evil spirits / sand dunes)

For thousands of years, visitors to some deserts around the world were confused at times. They heard loud, low, **rumbling** noises coming from sand **dunes** in these places. Not
5 knowing why or how this was happening, people were frightened by the sounds. Marco Polo, the great thirteenth-century Italian explorer, believed evil spirits were responsible.

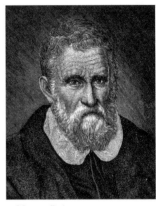

▲ Marco Polo

P2 _____ and how often singing sand occurs

These noises are frequently referred to as singing sand. This
10 **phenomenon** does not occur in every desert. In fact, there are only around thirty-five places worldwide known to produce singing sand. The noise produced can last for about a quarter of an hour. Some sand dunes create sound multiple times a day while others make noise less frequently. It is so loud that people ten kilometers away can hear it. In recent years, some
15 scientists have conducted research on singing sand and learned very much about it.

P3 Which (circumstances / temperatures) are needed for singing sand to occur

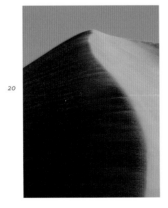

They have determined that certain circumstances must exist for sand to sing. First, the wind must be still, and the sand must be hot and dry. Next, sand must **accumulate** at the top
20 of a dune until the angle of the slope is around thirty-five degrees. When this takes place, a natural **avalanche** occurs, and sand begins **tumbling** down. The result is singing sand.

25 Singing sand does not sound the same everywhere. The **pitch** can be high or low depending upon where the dune is. Some scientists examined

▲ Singing sand dunes

the sand in dunes in Morocco and Oman which created singing sand. They learned that the Moroccan sand produced sound at around 105 Hertz while the Omani sand ranged from ninety to 150 Hertz. A close analysis revealed that the Moroccan grains of sand were nearly **identical** in size. The Omani <u>ones</u> varied greatly in size.

³⁰

Scientists speculate that as sand moves down a dune, individual grains **collide** with one another. While a single collision would not produce an **audible** sound, millions of collisions produce sound people can clearly hear. Words 319

P4 What scientists revealed about why singing sand produces different

P5 What scientists (know / speculate) about the causes of singing sand

i The noise created by singing sand can be extremely loud in some deserts. It could cause hearing damage to a person listening to it for more than fifteen minutes. The loudest singing sand happens in the Badain Jaran Desert in China. It has sand dunes almost 500 meters high.

Check the main point of the passage.

a. Singing sand has been heard by people for thousands of years.

b. Singing sand only happens in around thirty-five places around the world.

c. Scientists believe they know why singing sand happens in some deserts.

d. More research needs to be done for scientists to understand singing sand.

Reading Comprehension

1 **Why does the author mention Marco Polo?**

    a. To call him one of the past's greatest explorers

    b. To state his thoughts on what causes singing sand

    c. To point out some of the places that he visited

    d. To argue that he was the first explorer who heard singing sand

2 **In paragraph 2, all of the following questions are answered EXCEPT:**

    a. Up to how long does singing sand last?

    b. How frequently does singing sand occur in some places?

    c. Where have scientists studied singing sand recently?

    d. In how many places around the world can singing sand be heard?

3 **The word circumstances in the passage is closest in meaning to**

    a. noises   b. places   c. conditions   d. formations

4 **What does the underlined part in the passage mean?**

    a. sounds   b. grains of sand   c. pitches   d. sand dunes

5 **According to the passage, which of the following is NOT true about singing sand?**

    a. The pitch it creates is usually very low.

    b. Hot and dry sand is necessary for sand to sing.

    c. It does not sound the same in different places.

    d. The sizes of the grains of sand can affect the pitch of the sounds.

6 **How loud is singing sand?**

Singing sand is so loud that _____.

7 **What happens when the angle of a slope of a sand dune is thirty-five degrees?**

_____

Organizing the Passage

Complete the organizer with the phrases in the box.

Singing Sand

What It Is	• It has been heard by people in deserts for ❶_____. • Only around thirty-five places in the world produce singing sand. • It can make a ❷_____ for about a quarter of an hour, and people ten kilometers away can hear it.
Necessary Circumstances	• The wind must be still, and the sand must be ❸_____. • The sand at the top of the dune must create a slope with an angle that is ❹_____.
Singing Sand Sounds	• The pitch of the sounds can be high or low. • Scientists learned that sand in ❺_____ deserts created different sounds. • They found out that the Moroccan grains of sand were similar in size while the Omani ones were not. • They think the ❻_____ with one another produce sound.

low, rumbling sound	collisions of grains of sand	hot and dry
thousands of years	Moroccan and Omani	thirty-five degrees

Summarizing the Passage

Use the phrases in the box to complete the summary.

	different sounds	sand falls down
the wind is still	around the world	grains of sand

People have been hearing low, rumbling sounds in some deserts for thousands of years. This singing sand only happens in around thirty-five places ❶_____. Scientists have done some research on it recently. They learned that singing sand happens when ❷_____, and the sand is hot and dry. When ❸_____ the dune, it creates sound. But the pitches can be different. Scientists speculate that the sizes of the grains of sand cause ❹_____. When falling sand collides with other ❺_____, it makes singing sand.

Geology

Unit 6
Volcanic Eruptions

Think about the Topic

1 Do you think all volcanoes erupt the same way?

2 What causes a volcano to erupt?

Vocabulary Preview

A **Match the words with their definitions by writing the correct letters in the blanks.**

1 eruption _____   a. to see; to notice

2 destructive _____   b. to destroy completely

3 spew _____   c. the explosion of a volcano

4 ash _____   d. with people or animals living there

5 lava _____   e. able to flow or move like water

6 fluid _____   f. to shoot out, often quickly or violently

7 inhabited _____   g. causing a great amount of damage

8 observe _____   h. the soft gray powder shot out by a volcano

9 consume _____   i. molten rock that flows out from a volcano

10 obliterate _____   j. to destroy by burning or by covering with water, ash, etc.

B **Choose the words that have similar** (*sim.*) **or opposite** (*opp.*) **meanings from the box.**

explode	create	solid

1 fluid _____ *opp.*

2 burst _____ *sim.*

3 obliterate _____ *opp.*

Background Knowledge

A volcano is a place on the Earth where a crack in the crust allows heated rock to rise to the surface. The rock is called magma and is so hot that it is melted. When there is enough pressure underground, magma, as well as gas, ash, and rocks, rises to the surface. Then, it is expelled from the volcano.

Volcanic Eruptions

Q

What is each paragraph mainly about?

P1 What volcanoes can do and how _____ they can be

P2 What the (characteristics / appearances) of a Hawaiian eruption are

P3 What _____ eruptions are like

P4 How (common / violent) and explosive Plinian eruptions are

Volcanic **eruptions** are some of nature's most **destructive** forces. They can **spew** large amounts of gas, **ash**, rocks, and **lava** into the air. Some, like the one at Mount Tambora in 1815, have been so powerful that they affected the global climate. Not all volcanoes erupt in the same way though. 5 Geologists have identified several types of eruptions.

One is the Hawaiian eruption. It is named after Mount Kilauea, a volcano in Hawaii. It results in lava being ejected high into the air. Called lava fountains, streams of lava can rise more than 300 meters high. A Hawaiian eruption can last for long periods of time—even for years. The lava ejected 10 during it is very **fluid**, so it can flow great distances before stopping.

Some volcanoes shoot large amounts of lava hundreds of meters high, yet they do not erupt continually. Instead, they erupt every few minutes. These are Strombolian eruptions. They are named after Stromboli, a volcano in Italy. The reason a volcano erupts in this manner is that the magma 15 inside it has large bubbles of gas. When they burst, they expel lava at great force. They are explosive but not too violent. Still, Strombolian eruptions can be dangerous if they take place near **inhabited** areas.

Plinian eruptions are some of the most violent and explosive. 20 They were first **observed** by Pliny the Younger, a Roman. In 79 A.D., he saw the eruption of Mount Vesuvius, which **consumed** the nearby city Pompeii. Plinian

▲ Lava flows

25 eruptions can shoot gas and ash fifty kilometers into the sky. They can shoot lava that lands several kilometers away. They also create

▲ A Strombolian eruption

pyroclastic flows. These are fast-moving masses of gas, lava, rock, and ash. They **obliterate** anything in their way. In 1980, Mount St. Helens, an American volcano, erupted in this manner.

There are many other types of eruptions. Yet Hawaiian, Strombolian, and Plinian eruptions are among the most explosive and noticeable. *30* **Words 319**

i Large volcanic eruptions can send ash shooting high into the atmosphere. This ash can remain in the air for a long time. It often blocks the sun's rays, which can cause the global temperature to decline. This can result in global cooling for a period of time.

 Check the main idea of the passage.

a. Volcanic eruptions can cause large amounts of damage.

b. There are many ways that volcanoes can erupt.

c. Volcanoes only exist in a few places on the Earth.

d. Most volcanoes have Hawaiian or Strombolian eruptions.

Reading Comprehension

1 Why does the author mention Mount Tambora?

    a. To explain what kind of eruption it made

    b. To mention that it erupted in a unique way

    c. To explain how powerfully it once erupted

    d. To mention what it spewed when it erupted

2 In paragraph 2, which of the following is mentioned about Hawaiian eruptions?

    a. How often they erupt

    b. How they can create new islands

    c. How much damage they can do

    d. How high they can shoot lava

3 The word expel in the passage is closest in meaning to

    a. heat   b. produce   c. look after   d. shoot out

4 According to the passage, which of the following is true about Strombolian eruptions?

    a. They are the most violent eruptions.

    b. They expel large amounts of lava continually.

    c. They shoot lava hundreds of meters high.

    d. The lava from them flows long distances before it stops.

5 In paragraph 4, which of the following can be inferred about Plinian eruptions?

    a. They are the most common type of eruption.

    b. They can cause great amounts of damage.

    c. They only happened during ancient times.

    d. They are less destructive than Strombolian eruptions.

6 How long can a Hawaiian eruption last?

    It can last for _____.

7 Why does a Strombolian eruption erupt every few minutes?

    _____

Organizing the Passage

Select the appropriate statements from the answer choices and match them to the eruption to which they relate. Two of the answer choices will NOT be used.

Hawaiian Eruption	Strombolian Eruption	Plinian Eruption
•	•	•
•	•	•
	•	

1 It gets its name from a volcano in Italy.

2 It can produce lava fountains 300 meters high.

3 The eruption of Mount Vesuvius was this kind of eruption.

4 It ejects fluid lava that can flow great distances.

5 The Mount Tambora eruption was a violent example of it.

6 It erupts every few minutes.

7 It can produce fast-moving masses of gas, lava, ash, and rock.

8 It has killed more people than any other type of eruption recently.

9 It is not violent even though it is explosive.

Summarizing the Passage

Use the phrases in the box to complete the summary.

> types of eruptions   create pyroclastic flows
> explosive eruptions   flows great distances   gas and ash

Volcanic eruptions spew gas, ash, rocks, and lava into the air. There are several

❶_____ . The Hawaiian eruption can continually shoot lava streams into the air

for years. This lava is fluid, so it ❷_____ . Strombolian eruptions shoot lava into

the air, but they erupt every few minutes. They are ❸_____ but are not violent.

Plinian eruptions were noticed by Pliny the Younger when he saw Mount Vesuvius erupt.

These shoot ❹_____ high into the air. They ❺_____ that destroy

everything in their way, too.

Chapter 4
Economics

Economics refers to the study of the manufacture, distribution, and usage of both goods and services. Economists study markets and how buyers and sellers act. They look back in history to learn about the economic conditions in the past and how they may apply to the present and the future.

Unit 7
Cottage Industries

Think about the Topic

1 Where do you think people in the past created goods?

2 How do people create goods today?

Vocabulary Preview

A **Match the words with their definitions by writing the correct letters in the blanks.**

1 engage in _____ a. to make something on a large scale

2 textile _____ b. to be involved in; to take part in

3 mass-produce _____ c. to focus on one thing that one is good at

4 sew _____ d. a person who provides food for others

5 necessity _____ e. something that a person need to have

6 standard (*n.*) _____ f. to use a needle and thread to join with stitches

7 assembly line _____ g. not making good use of time, money, or material

8 specialize in _____ h. cloth or clothing made by knitting or weaving

9 inefficient _____ i. a level of quality regarded as usual or normal for its type

10 caterer _____ j. a grouping of machines in which each person does one job before passing an item to the next person

B **Choose the words that have similar (*sim.*) or opposite (*opp.*) meanings from the box.**

	seller	plant	pretty

1 factory _____ *sim.*

2 fairly _____ *sim.*

3 buyer _____ *opp.*

Background Knowledge

For centuries, most people produced the goods that they needed in their homes. People such as blacksmiths worked with metal items while weavers made clothing and other similar items. Few people had the special skills needed to make these items, so they were often expensive. This only changed when the Industrial Revolution began around the year 1700.

Cottage Industries

Q

What is each paragraph mainly about?

 What happened after the _____ started

P2 (Where / What) cottage industries are

P3 Some _____ of cottage industries

P4 How cottage industries (helped / hurt) people

In the 1700s, the Industrial Revolution started in England and then spread to other countries. During it, people began to use machines to do work. This let factories be created. In them, people **engaged in** the mass production of **textiles** and other products. Today, the majority of goods
5 around the world are **mass-produced** in factories. Prior to the Industrial Revolution, they were made on a much _____ scale.

For centuries, most people made goods in their homes or in small shops near their homes. These were known as cottage industries. A cottage is a small home. Since items were made in people's homes, that is how the
10 name cottage industry was created. People did all kinds of work in cottage industries. Many people made cloth or **sewed** clothes. Others made leather goods, bricks, nails, and numerous other **necessities**.

Cottage industries had a number of disadvantages. There were no **standards**, so the items made varied in quality and size. Since one person
15 made the entire item, manufacturing was a very slow process. This was different from today's **assembly lines**, where workers **specialize in** specific tasks, making the manufacturing process fast. The prices of goods were fairly high, too.

On the other hand, cottage industries provided some benefits. They let
20 people work out of their homes, which was convenient. People also did not have to spend large amounts of money starting business since they were so small. Cottage industries also provided jobs, which helped local economies.

Once the Industrial Revolution began, most cottage industries disappeared. They were too slow and **inefficient** to be competitive with factories. But some of them still exist today. Most involve the textile industry. Food providers such as bakers and **caterers** also operate as cottage industries. Thanks to the Internet, which lets people sell to buyers around the world, it is once again possible for cottage industries to thrive.

Words 311

²⁵ P5 What types of cottage industries still _____ today

i During the Industrial Revolution, people began using water power and steam power to operate machines. This led to the rise of factories. Many cottage industries disappeared because they could not compete with the cheap goods factories made.

 Check the main point of the passage.

a. A lot of people worked in cottage industries in the past.

b. Most cottage industries made goods of poor quality.

c. Cottage industries had advantages and disadvantages.

d. There are very few cottage industries nowadays.

Reading Comprehension

1 What is the best choice for the blank?

    a. better   b. smaller   c. more expensive   d. larger

2 In paragraph 2, which of the following is NOT mentioned about cottage industries?

    a. How they got their name

    b. How people felt about them

    c. How long they were used by people

    d. What types of goods people made with them

3 According to paragraph 3, which of the following is true about cottage industries?

    a. They charged low prices.

    b. They had standards for making items.

    c. They could not make items very fast.

    d. They used high-quality materials.

4 Why does the author mention jobs?

    a. To describe an advantage of cottage industries

    b. To focus on the lack of training they required

    c. To claim that people with them worked long hours

    d. To discuss how well paid those in cottage industries were

5 The word thrive in the passage is closest in meaning to

    a. exist   b. advertise   c. succeed   d. sell

6 Why did most cottage industries disappear once the Industrial Revolution began?

    They were too _____.

7 What kinds of cottage industries still exist today?

    _____

Organizing the Passage

Complete the organizer with the phrases in the box.

<table>
<tr><td colspan="2" align="center">Cottage Industries</td></tr>
<tr>
<td>The Industrial Revolution</td>
<td>
• It ❶_____ in the 1700s and then spread to other countries.
• It resulted in people working in factories to ❷_____.
</td>
</tr>
<tr>
<td>What Cottage Industries Are</td>
<td>
• Before ❸_____, people made all kinds of goods in their homes in cottage industries.
• People made cloth, sewed clothes, and made leather goods, bricks, nails, and other necessities.
</td>
</tr>
<tr>
<td>Disadvantages</td>
<td>
• There were ❹_____, so the items varied in quality and size.
• Making goods was a slow process, and the prices of goods were very high.
</td>
</tr>
<tr>
<td>Advantages</td>
<td>
• People could work out of their homes and did not need ❺_____ to start businesses.
• ❻_____ were helped by the jobs they provided.
</td>
</tr>
</table>

mass-produce goods	a lot of money	the Industrial Revolution
started in England	local economies	no standards

Summarizing the Passage

The first sentence of a short summary is provided below. Complete the summary by choosing THREE answer choices that express the most important ideas.

> People in the past relied on cottage industries to manufacture goods.

1 Nowadays, there are very few cottage industries except in the food service industry.

2 The Industrial Revolution began in the 1700s and changed how people made goods.

3 It was cheap and easy to start cottage industries, and they also provided jobs for people.

4 People once made all kinds of products, such as clothes and leather goods, in their homes or in small shops near their homes.

5 Making goods in cottage industries was a slow, expensive process, and there were no standards for goods.

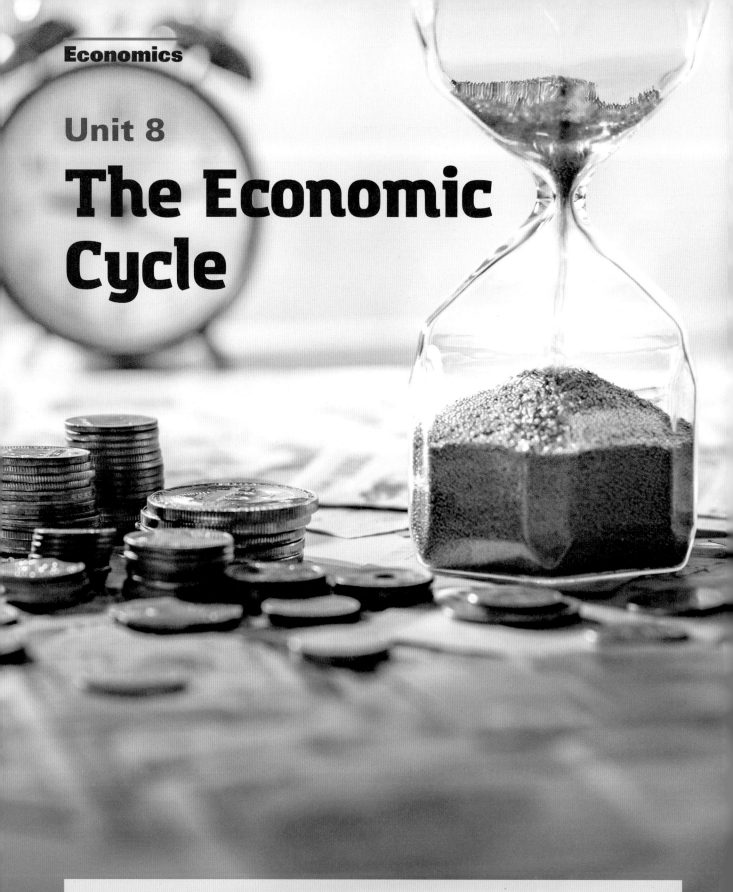

Unit 8
The Economic Cycle

Think about the Topic

1   What do you think the economic cycle is?

2   What happens during good economies and bad economies?

Vocabulary Preview

A   **Match the words with their definitions by writing the correct letters in the blanks.**

1 stage   _____   a. to become smaller

2 boom   _____   b. one step in a process

3 investment   _____   c. to improve or increase rapidly

4 salary   _____   d. the number of people not having a job

5 unemployment   _____   e. a time when the prices of goods are rising

6 inflation   _____   f. the state of not being able to pay one's debts

7 rate   _____   g. money a person borrows that must be paid back

8 loan   _____   h. an amount of money a person makes for doing a job

9 shrink   _____   i. the spending of money in order to make a profit

10 bankruptcy   _____   j. the amount of a charge or payment that must be made

B   **Choose the words that have similar** (*sim.*) **or opposite** (*opp.*) **meanings from the box.**

positive	loss	shrink

1 expand   _____ *opp.*

2 confident   _____ *sim.*

3 profit   _____ *opp.*

Background Knowledge

A country's economy is constantly changing. It sometimes experiences good times and sometimes goes through bad times. The lengths of these good and bad times vary, but all economies go through them. Economists can use their knowledge of the economic cycle to predict what is going to happen to a country's economy.

The Economic Cycle

Q

What is each paragraph mainly about?

P1 What the _____ of the economic cycle are

P2 The characteristics of the (economic / expansion) stage

P3 What happens during a _____

P4 The causes and effects of a (recession / depression)

Each country's economy undergoes changes. These can be positive or negative. Economists have identified several **stages** economies go through. They are expansion, slowdown, recession, and recovery. Together, they are called the economic cycle or business cycle.

5   In the expansion stage, an economy grows. Certain conditions exist to make an economy **boom**. For instance, people open new businesses while the stock market sees lots of **investment**. Workers' **salaries** increase. There is low **unemployment** since so many new jobs are _____. Individuals also feel confident in the economy, which

10 helps it improve.

Economies do not expand constantly though. At some point, a slowdown happens. While the economy is still getting larger, it is not doing so at a rapid pace. During a slowdown, consumer confidence falls. People spend less and save more. Prices of goods rise, resulting in **inflation**. Interest

15 **rates** rise, too, making fewer people apply for **loans**. This results in less investment, so the stock market declines. Finally, businesses stop hiring people, and unemployment rises.

When an economy **shrinks**, a recession occurs. This is a period when an economy gets smaller for at least six months. A stock market

20 crash, multiple bank failures, or a major terrorist attack can start a recession. During one, unemployment rises, and so do **bankruptcies**. Consumer confidence declines, which makes people spend less. Governments often run deficits since they increase spending to try to help the economy. A

25 recession lasting for two or more years is called a depression.

Finally, a recession ends, and the economy gets better during a recovery. Companies make profits and hire more workers. Because people have jobs, they spend more money. Interest rates are low, so people borrow more and invest in the stock market.

P5 The results of a
_____

30

The four stages of the economic cycle last for various amounts of time. Some last for months whereas others last for years. All economies go through each stage at some point. **Words 316**

> *i* Parts of the economic cycle can last for a long time. For instance, in the United States, there was a long boom period in the 1920s called the Roaring Twenties. However, the Great Depression followed soon afterward. It lasted more than a decade.

 Check what the passage is mainly about.

   a. The reasons economies have recessions

   b. The characteristics of an economic boom

   c. The best economies in modern history

   d. The different stages economies go through

Reading Comprehension

1 What is the best choice for the blank?

a. improved   b. created   c. considered   d. lost

2 The word rapid in the passage is closest in meaning to

a. swift   b. powerful   c. effective   d. obvious

3 According to paragraph 3, which of the following is NOT true about a slowdown?

a. The stock market goes down.

b. Inflation takes place during it.

c. Fewer people get new jobs.

d. Interest rates decline.

4 Why does the author mention A stock market crash?

a. To state that it happens frequently

b. To claim that it can destroy an economy

c. To argue that it is worse than a terrorist attack

d. To name one possible cause of a recession

5 Which of the following is NOT true according to the passage?

a. Workers' salaries go up in the expansion stage.

b. Consumer confidence falls during a slowdown.

c. A recovery happens after a recession ends.

d. Governments reduce spending during a recession.

6 What are the four stages economies go through?

The four stages are _____ .

7 What is a depression?

_____

Organizing the Passage

Complete the organizer with the phrases in the box.

The Economic Cycle

Expansion	• It takes place when ❶_____. • People open new businesses and invest in the stock market. • Unemployment is low, and people ❷_____ in the economy.
Slowdown	• The economy gets better but at a slower pace than during an expansion. • People ❸_____, so they save more and spend less. • Inflation takes place. And there are ❹_____, which result in less investment.
Recession	• This happens when an economy gets smaller for at least six months. • Both unemployment and ❺_____ while consumer confidence declines.
Recovery	• The economy improves while companies ❻_____. • People spend more money, and they also invest in the stock market.

higher interest rates   are confident   are less confident

make profits   an economy grows   bankruptcies increase

Summarizing the Passage

Use the phrases in the box to complete the summary.

spend more money   the expansion stage

gets smaller   consumer confidence falls   lose their jobs

There are four stages in the economic cycle: expansion, slowdown, recession, and recovery. An economy grows during ❶_____. People are confident in the economy, have jobs, and are making more money. When a slowdown occurs, an economy improves more slowly while ❷_____. This leads to a recession, which is a time when the economy ❸_____ for six months or more. People ❹_____ and are less confident in the economy. When a recession ends, a recovery begins. More people get hired as companies make profits. People can ❺_____ and invest as well.

Chapter 5
Technology

Technology refers to the knowledge, methods, and ways of making various items. Technology often involves the use of machines and is constantly being improved through various discoveries and inventions. Thanks to technology, modern engineering, medicine, construction, and other fields have improved greatly.

Unit 9

Modern Surveillance Societies

Think about the Topic

1 How often do you think you are caught on security cameras per day?

2 Do you think it is right for governments to observe people all the time?

Vocabulary Preview

A **Match the words with their definitions by writing the correct letters in the blanks.**

1 surveillance _____ a. covering very much

2 violate _____ b. to collect; to gather

3 privacy _____ c. to move around in a circle

4 satellite _____ d. going in, often without permission

5 orbit _____ e. to watch carefully over a period of time

6 comprehensive _____ f. to take away or disturb something illegally

7 monitor _____ g. the constant watching of a person or place

8 intrusive _____ h. to end or remove, such as a law or rule

9 amass _____ i. a machine that goes around the Earth, moon, sun, or other body

10 repeal _____ j. the state of being free from being observed or bothered by others

B **Choose the words that have similar** (*sim.*) **or opposite** (*opp.*) **meanings from the box.**

allowed	trace	limited

1 comprehensive _____ *opp.*

2 track _____ *sim.*

3 legal _____ *sim.*

Background Knowledge

Closed-circuit television systems, or CCTV, are a modern form of surveillance. Shops use them to monitor customers to reduce theft. Homeowners have them to protect their homes from being robbed. They are also used on roads to spot accidents and have been used to find missing people as well. However, some people say that CCTV cameras are creating surveillance societies.

Modern Surveillance Societies

Q

What is each paragraph mainly about?

P1 (Why / How) there is mass surveillance in some countries

P2 What types of _____ are used thanks to modern digital technology

P3 What mass surveillance is like in London and _____

P4 How other countries have made the gathering of information (legal / illegal)

These days, the mass **surveillance** of people is common in some countries. Governments claim they are doing so to prevent terrorism as well as crime. But people often complain that the various actions are **violating** their right to **privacy**.

5 Modern digital technology has made mass surveillance possible. In some cities, cameras are in apartments, stores, and offices, and even on city streets. They record everything all day and night long. There are **satellites orbiting** high above the Earth. They take pictures clear enough to make out people's faces. Phone calls and Internet usage can be tracked and 10 recorded. Even the locations of people's cellphones can be traced. So it is possible to tell where their owners are.

At present, England and China have the world's most **comprehensive** mass-surveillance societies. London, England, has more than half a million 15 security cameras keeping watch over it. It is difficult to walk anywhere in the city without being caught on camera. In China, there are more than 200 million security cameras. The government also controls access to the 20 Internet. Anybody who goes online can be **monitored**. When users log on to certain websites, they are cut off from the Internet.

Other countries have similar— 25 but less **intrusive**—systems in place. These include the United States and

many countries in Europe. They have laws which make gathering all of the information legal. This lets agencies like the American NSA and FBI watch over citizens.

Many people say that they have lost their privacy. They point out that governments have **amassed** too much power. They are also upset since they never voted to make <u>these activities</u> be legal. People are afraid that they are losing their freedom. So many groups and individuals have been fighting back against surveillance states. They are trying to get many laws **repealed**. They hope that people will get their privacy back one day.

30 🄿🄳 What people
_____ back against mass surveillance are saying and doing

Words 312

> ℹ One place where surveillance has increased is in airports. There are numerous cameras in airports. Travelers must often undergo intrusive security checks of themselves and their baggage. In addition, facial-recognition cameras take passengers' pictures and their fingerprints are often collected.

 Check the main point of the passage.

a. Cameras are used to observe people's actions all around the world.

b. Modern digital technology has enabled the rise of surveillance states.

c. England and China are the two biggest surveillance states in the world.

d. Many people are trying to reduce the power of surveillance states.

Reading Comprehension

1 In paragraph 2, all of the following questions are answered EXCEPT:

   a. Where have cameras been placed in some cities?

   b. What can be traced on people's cellphones?

   c. How clear are the pictures that some satellites can take?

   d. Which countries collect the images captured by cameras and satellites?

2 The word they in the passage refers to

   a. 200 million security cameras

   b. the government

   c. users

   d. certain websites

3 The word gathering in the passage is closest in meaning to

   a. collecting   b. observing   c. meeting   d. studying

4 Which of the following is true according to the passage?

   a. Certain websites are banned in England.

   b. The Chinese government can watch what people do online.

   c. Every major city in England and China has millions of security cameras.

   d. Many European countries are banning gathering information by law.

5 What does the underlined part in the passage mean?

   a. the protection of people's right to privacy

   b. the repealing of laws allowing mass surveillance

   c. actions resulting in mass surveillance of people

   d. the forming of agencies such as the NSA and the FBI

6 What is it difficult to do in London, England?

   It is difficult to _____ .

7 How are many groups and individuals fighting back against surveillance states?

   _____

Organizing the Passage

Complete the organizer with the phrases in the box.

Modern Surveillance Societies	
Modern Digital Technology	• It allows cameras in cities to record everything they see ❶_____ . • ❷_____ the Earth can take clear pictures, and people's cellphones can be traced.
London and China	• They have the world's most comprehensive mass-surveillance societies. • London has more than ❸_____ cameras watching people. • China has more than 200 million security cameras. • The Chinese government also controls access to the Internet and ❹_____ .
Complaints about Mass Surveillance	• People say that they have lost their privacy and that governments have ❺_____ . • They fear they are ❻_____ , so they are fighting back. • They are trying to get many laws repealed to get their privacy back.

> satellites orbiting   monitors online activity   all day and night long
> losing their freedom   too much power   half a million

Summarizing the Passage

Use the phrases in the box to complete the summary.

> many laws repealed   controls Internet access
> observing people   watch over citizens   are also traced

The mass surveillance of people has increased all around the world. There are cameras ❶_____ in cities and satellites that take pictures from high above the Earth. People's cellphones ❷_____ . England and China have the most comprehensive mass-surveillance societies. There are security cameras everywhere in London. The Chinese government uses cameras and ❸_____ , too. Other countries have laws making it legal to ❹_____ . Some people are fighting back against surveillance states. They are trying to get ❺_____ .

Unit 10

Deep-Sea Vehicles

Think about the Topic

1 What kinds of vehicles can go deep beneath the ocean?

2 Why do people want to go to the bottom of the ocean?

Vocabulary Preview

A **Match the words with their definitions by writing the correct letters in the blanks.**

1 intense   _____   a. a ship or large boat

2 arguably   _____   b. to disconnect; to take off

3 manned   _____   c. able to run or operate by itself

4 illuminate   _____   d. to make bright; to provide light

5 free-fall   _____   e. existing at a high degree or amount

6 detach   _____   f. possibly being debated or challenged

7 sediment   _____   g. requiring a person to use or operate

8 vessel   _____   h. to go down due only to the effects of gravity

9 sonar   _____   i. a way to detect underwater objects by using sound

10 autonomous   _____   j. sand, dirt, and other small particles at the bottom of a body of water

B **Choose the words that have similar** (*sim.*) **or opposite** (*opp.*) **meanings from the box.**

enable	information	darken

1 illuminate   _____ *opp.*

2 permit   _____ *sim.*

3 data   _____ *sim.*

Background Knowledge

There are five oceans on the Earth: the Atlantic, Pacific, Indian, Arctic, and Antarctic oceans. These oceans are all connected to one another and cover around seventy percent of the Earth's surface. More than eighty percent of the Earth's oceans has not been mapped or explored. Scientists therefore have much to learn about the mysteries of the oceans.

Deep-Sea Vehicles

Q

What is each paragraph mainly about?

P1 How deep the oceans are and why it is difficult to (explore / travel on) them

P2 What _____ is able to do

P3 How *Medea* and *Jason* are able to _____ places

The Earth's five oceans cover more than seventy percent of the surface of the planet. The average depth of the oceans is around 3,600 meters. The deepest place on the Earth, Challenger Deep in the Mariana Trench, is around 11,000 meters deep. Due to the great _____ and
5 **intense** pressure far beneath the surface, exploring the deep sea is difficult. That is changing though as some vehicles are permitting people to travel to the bottom of the ocean.

Arguably the most famous is the **manned** deep-sea vehicle *Deepsea Challenger*. ❶ Able to carry one person, it reached the bottom of Challenger
10 Deep. ❷ They can **illuminate** objects thirty meters away. *Deepsea Challenger* is lighter than water. ❸ So weights must be attached for it to dive. ❹ To go down, it **free-falls** to the bottom. When the pilot wants to resurface, he **detaches** the weights. The vehicle can collect rock, **sediment**, and biological samples. It has multiple recording devices, too.
15 On its voyages, it has made numerous discoveries of the deep sea.

Another type of vehicle is the remotely operated vehicle, or ROV. *Medea* and *Jason* are two of these. These unmanned vehicles are designed to work together. A pilot on the surface controls them through a cable 10 kilometers long that connects the **vessels**. *Medea*
20 receives the signals. It illuminates, controls, and records the actions of *Jason*. Meanwhile, *Jason* collects data from its **sonar** system, cameras, and

◄ An autonomous underwater vehicle

74

▲ A remotely operated vehicle

robotic arms. They have stayed underwater for as long as seven days and have explored places around the world.

25

There are other types of deep-sea vehicles, including AUVs, **autonomous** underwater vehicles. These machines are programmed to operate all by themselves without any humans. They are being used by scientists to reveal the mysteries of the deep sea. Thanks to them, more and more is being learned about the world beneath the water each year. Words 315

P4 (Where / What) AUVs are and what they can do

i In March 2012, world-famous movie director James Cameron descended to the bottom of Challenger Deep. He traveled in *Deepsea Challenger* and became the second person to descend that far beneath the Earth's surface.

 Check what the passage is mainly about.

a. The most unique places that are located deep underwater

b. The different types of vehicles used to explore the deep sea

c. The difficulties involved in going to the bottom of the ocean

d. The underwater discoveries that scientists are making

Reading Comprehension

1 What is the best choice for the blank?

    a. depths   b. distance   c. temperature   d. danger

2 Where would the following sentence best fit in paragraph 2?

It has strong batteries and powerful lights.

    a. ❶   b. ❷   c. ❸   d. ❹

3 According to paragraphs 1 and 2, which of the following is NOT true about *Deepsea Challenger*?

    a. It went down to the deepest place on the Earth.

    b. It is able to collect a variety of samples.

    c. Two people can travel in it at the same time.

    d. Weights are used to make it go to the bottom of the ocean.

4 In paragraph 3, which of the following can be inferred about *Medea* and *Jason*?

    a. They failed when trying to explore some places.

    b. One of them cannot work without the other.

    c. A pilot must board *Medea* in order to control *Jason*.

    d. They are better known than *Deepsea Challenger*.

5 The word them in the passage refers to

    a. these machines

    b. humans

    c. scientists

    d. the mysteries of the deep sea

6 What is the deepest place on the Earth?

The deepest place on the Earth is _____.

7 What does *Medea* do?

_____

Organizing the Passage

Complete the organizer with the phrases in the box.

Deep-sea Vehicles

Deepsea Challenger	• It is an unmanned deep-sea vehicle. • It has traveled to ❶_____ on the Earth. • It has lots of ❷_____ and can collect samples.
Medea and *Jason*	• They are remotely operated vehicles. • They are controlled ❸_____ by a person ❹_____. • They have visited places ❺_____.
AUVs	• It is an ❻_____ vehicle. • Scientists use it to reveal many mysteries of the world beneath the water.

recording devices	on the surface	around the world
autonomous underwater	through a long cable	the deepest place

Summarizing the Passage

Use the phrases in the box to complete the summary.

biological samples	remotely operated
reveal the mysteries	a manned vehicle	the Earth's surface

The oceans cover most of ❶_____ and average 3,600 meters in depth. So exploring them is difficult. Some deep-sea vehicles are letting people visit the bottom of the ocean though. *Deepsea Challenger* is ❷_____ that has reached the bottom of Challenger Deep. It can free-fall to the bottom and collect rock, sediment, and ❸_____. *Medea* and *Jason* are ❹_____ vehicles. They work together and can stay underwater for as long as seven days. AUVs are autonomous underwater vehicles. Scientists are using them to ❺_____ of the deep sea.

Chapter **6**
Zoology

Zoology refers to the study of animals. Zoologists study the bodies of animals as well as their habits and habitats. They often try to learn how animals interact with other animals and their ecosystems.

Unit 11

Bird Feathers

Think about the Topic

1 What kinds of feathers do you think birds have?

2 How do feathers help birds?

Vocabulary Preview

A **Match the words with their definitions by writing the correct letters in the blanks.**

1 evolve _____ a. very important

2 bend _____ b. soft and very light

3 strike _____ c. nice or clean looking

4 neat _____ d. to change slowly over time

5 vital _____ e. to hit, often very strongly

6 fluffy _____ f. the outline or edge of something

7 contour _____ g. the purpose that something has

8 sting _____ h. focused on one particular thing

9 specialized _____ i. to change in shape from straight to curved

10 function _____ j. the act of stabbing with a sharp, pointed object

B **Choose the words that have similar (*sim.*) or opposite (*opp.*) meanings from the box.**

bed	form	bendable

1 shape _____ *sim.*

2 mattress _____ *sim.*

3 stiff _____ *opp.*

Background Knowledge

The feathers of birds give them their unique appearance. Thanks to them, birds appear in many colors. However, feathers have more uses than just decoration. They enable birds to fly and also help them stay warm. This is possible because of how different feathers have developed over time.

Bird Feathers

Q

What is each paragraph mainly about?

 What feathers are and (where / how) they evolved

P2 How _____ feathers help birds

P3 What the locations and (purposes / sizes) of down feathers are

P4 What semiplumes and _____ do for birds

The only animals with feathers are birds. Feathers are similar to hair since they grow from the skin. Bird feathers have **evolved** over millions of years, which has led to the creation of several different types of feathers. These feathers come in a wide variety of shapes, sizes, and colors, and
5 they also have different purposes.

Among the most important of bird feathers are called contour feathers. These are the largest feathers and include flight feathers and tail feathers. Contour feathers give birds their shape and color. They must be light and strong to enable birds to achieve flight, so they frequently **bend** as birds fly
10 but rarely break. They also provide protection from the sun, wind, rain, and any physical objects that **strike** birds.

Down feathers, which lack the **neat** appearance of contour feathers, are also **vital** to birds. These soft, **fluffy** feathers are found beneath contour feathers. They help keep birds warm and dry, so they are of particular
15 importance to water birds such as ducks, geese, and swans. These feathers have been collected by people for centuries to use in pillows and mattresses thanks to their softness.

Semiplumes are a combination of **contour** feathers and down feathers. They are located between contour feathers and provide insulation for birds while also helping give them their shape. Yet another
20 of the important bird feathers are called bristles. Not all birds have bristles, but they are located around the eyes and mouths of the birds that have them. These small, stiff feathers provide

▲ A woodpecker that has bristles around its beak

protection. For instance, birds that feed on bees and wasps have bristles to ₂₅ protect themselves from harmful **stings**.

There are other types of feathers, but those are four of the most important ones. Bird feathers have changed over time to have highly **specialized functions**. Thanks to them, birds can not only fly but can also keep warm, safe, and dry. Words 313

<aside>
The colors of bird feathers are important to some birds. For instance, male cardinals are bright red, which helps them attract females. Likewise, peacocks have bright, colorful feathers to attract peahens, which are not as colorful.
</aside>

 Check the main point of the passage.

a. Birds have several types of feathers, each of which has its own purposes.

b. Birds are the only animals in the world that have feathers on their bodies.

c. Without feathers, birds would not be able to fly or keep themselves warm.

d. The feathers of birds give them the unique appearances they are known for.

Reading Comprehension

1 In paragraph 1, which of the following can be inferred about feathers?

   a. They act as substitutes for skin on birds.

   b. They can be found on birds and other modern-day animals.

   c. They are mostly the same shapes and sizes for all birds.

   d. They were different in appearance millions of years ago.

2 In paragraph 2, which of the following is NOT mentioned about contour feathers?

   a. How many of them birds have

   b. From what they protect birds

   c. How they enable birds to fly

   d. What the two types of them are

3 Why does the author mention ducks, geese, and swans?

   a. To call them the most common water birds

   b. To emphasize their lack of bristle feathers

   c. To indicate the importance of down feathers to them

   d. To state that they have more down feathers than contour ones

4 Which of the following is NOT true according to the passage?

   a. Semiplumes help keep birds warm.

   b. Down feathers give birds their shape and color.

   c. People use down feathers in pillows and mattresses.

   d. Bristles are located around the eyes and mouths of birds.

5 The word them in the passage refers to

   a. bristles   b. the eyes   c. mouths   d. the birds

6 Why do birds that feed on bees and wasps have bristles?

They have bristles _____.

7 What are semiplumes?

_____

Organizing the Passage

Complete the organizer with the phrases in the box.

Types of Bird Feathers

Contour Feathers	• They are the biggest of all bird feathers. • They enable birds to ❶_____. • They can protect birds from the sun, wind, rain, and ❷_____ that hit them.
Down Feathers	• They are ❸_____ and are used in mattresses and pillows. • They keep water birds ❹_____.
Semiplumes	• They are a combination of two other types of feathers. • They ❺_____ and give them their shape.
Bristles	• They are located around the eyes and mouths of birds. • They are ❻_____.

small, stiff feathers	warm and dry	fly in the air
soft and fluffy	physical objects	insulate birds

Summarizing the Passage

Use the phrases in the box to complete the summary.

down feathers	from harmful stings	
their shape	tail feathers	let birds fly

Over millions of years, different types of feathers have evolved on birds. Contour feathers are large and include flight feathers and ❶_____. They can bend since they ❷_____. They protect birds from the sun, wind, rain, and physical objects. ❸_____ are soft and fluffy and keep birds warm and dry. Water birds such as ducks, geese, and swans have them. Semiplumes are found between contour feathers. They insulate birds and give them ❹_____. Some birds have stiff bristles around their eyes and mouths. Bristles protect these birds ❺_____.

Zoology

Unit 12
Walking Fish

Think about the Topic

1 How do you think fish are able to walk?

2 What other unusual abilities do some fish have?

Vocabulary Preview

A **Match the words with their definitions by writing the correct letters in the blanks.**

1 transition _____ a. to leave

2 lung _____ b. to have

3 utilize _____ c. a change

4 gill _____ d. to use

5 nostril _____ e. to take deep breaths of air

6 gulp _____ f. considerable; very large in degree

7 fin _____ g. one of the two openings of the nose

8 possess _____ h. an organ that lets people and animals breathe air

9 extensive _____ i. the organ that lets fish breathe oxygen in water

10 depart _____ j. an external organ on a fish that lets it swim or change directions

B **Choose the words that have similar** (*sim.*) **or opposite** (*opp.*) **meanings from the box.**

around	end	flood

1 originate _____ *opp.*

2 drought _____ *opp.*

3 approximately _____ *sim.*

Background Knowledge

There have been fish in the world's oceans for more than 450 million years. They were alive before the dinosaurs came and have survived long after the dinosaurs went extinct. Fish are cold-blooded animals. There are around 32,000 species of fish on the Earth. Fish use their gills to remove oxygen from the water. This lets them survive underwater.

Walking Fish

Q

What is each paragraph mainly about?

P1 The belief that life originated in the oceans and then made the _____ to land

P2 How lungfish are able to survive in the water and (on land / in the air)

P3 The characteristics of the _____

Many biologists believe life on the Earth originated in the oceans. Later, animals began making the **transition** to land. This required them to evolve to breathe air and to have the ability to move on land. Scientists have long sought evidence that this happened. They believe they may have found
5   it in the form of walking fish such as the lungfish, the snakehead, and the mudskipper.

Land animals require **lungs** to breathe air whereas fish **utilize gills** to remove oxygen from the water. The lungfish has lungs and gills, which allow it to survive in both places. Some species of lungfish have **nostrils**
10   while others breathe through their mouths by **gulping** air. On land, the lungfish uses its **fins** like arms and legs, which let it move.

Similar to the lungfish, the snakehead **possesses** lungs and can often be found migrating out of water in certain situations. For instance,
15   when the water it lives in lacks enough oxygen, it will travel across small areas of land in search of better conditions. Likewise, it migrates in times when droughts dry up the pond or lake it lives in. The snakehead
20   cannot actually walk but instead pushes itself or crawls like a snake. It also cannot survive on land for **extensive** periods of time.

▲ Snakehead

A third type of walking fish is the mudskipper, which spends approximately seventy-five percent of its life on land. ❶
These let the fish be very mobile on land as it can climb

◄ Mudskippers

▲ Lungfish

trees and even jump. ❷ The mudskipper is capable of moving faster on land ²⁵ than in the water. ❸ Some biologists claim it acts more like a land animal than a fish. ❹

🄿🄰 How the mudskipper can spend so much of its (day / life) on land

    All three fish can breathe air and have the ability to live on land. By studying them and other similar animals, biologists hope to understand how animals changed when they **departed** the water many years ago.   Words 321

i In many parts of Asia, the snakehead is a valuable food fish. However, in other places, such as the United States, it is an invasive species. It can reproduce very quickly, and as a predator, it often kills large numbers of native fish.

 Check what the passage is mainly about.

    a. How some animals can breathe both water and air

    b. Snakeheads and lungfish and their characteristics

    c. Some types of fish that are capable of living on land

    d. How animals learned to move from the ocean to the land

Reading Comprehension

1 The word it in the passage refers to
   a. air
   b. land
   c. evidence that this happened
   d. walking fish

2 In paragraph 2, it can be inferred that the lungfish
   a. has fins that look like the legs of animals
   b. is capable of breathing through its nostrils
   c. can grow to be larger than all other walking fish
   d. can use its lungs and gills on land at the same time

3 The word migrating in the passage is closest in meaning to
   a. living   b. wandering   c. climbing   d. communicating

4 Where would the following sentence best fit in paragraph 4?

Its front fins are highly developed and are similar to hands.

   a. ❶   b. ❷   c. ❸   d. ❹

5 According to paragraph 4, which of the following is true about the mudskipper?
   a. It prefers to live in water than on land.
   b. It is able to walk faster than it can swim.
   c. It has a highly developed pair of hands.
   d. It has been known to make nests in trees.

6 How does the lungfish move on land?
   The lungfish _____.

7 What will the snakehead do when the water it lives in lacks enough oxygen?

   _____

Organizing the Passage

Select the appropriate statements from the answer choices and match them to the walking fish to which they relate. Two of the answer choices will NOT be used.

Lungfish	Snakehead	Mudskipper
•	•	•
•	•	•
	•	

1. Has the abilities to jump in the air and to climb trees
2. Can breathe air through its mouth or nostril
3. Sometimes hunts animals that live on land for food
4. Cannot walk but must push itself on land like a snake
5. Spends more time on land than in the water
6. Is known to leave the water when its ponds dry up
7. Cannot live on the land for a long period of time
8. Is able to use its fins like they are arms and legs
9. Lays its eggs in nests that are located on land

Summarizing the Passage

Use the phrases in the box to complete the summary.

> like a snake   climb trees and jump
> both lungs and gills   land creatures   migrate on land

Scientists believe walking fish are evidence that animals evolved from being ocean creatures to ❶_____. The lungfish has ❷_____, so it can survive in water and on land. It can use its fins like arms and legs to move on land. The snakehead also has lungs. It can ❸_____ to find better living conditions. It crawls on the ground ❹_____. The mudskipper spends around seventy-five percent of its life on land. It can ❺_____. Biologists say that it acts more like a land animal than a fish.

Chapter 7
Journalism

Journalism refers to the act of reporting on and writing about the news. Journalists often publish their stories in newspapers or magazines. In modern times, they now publish on the Internet. Journalists may simply report news stories and describe events as they happened, or they may provide in-depth analysis of events.

Unit 13
Yellow Journalism and Muckraking

Think about the Topic

1 Do you think that yellow journalism and muckraking have positive or negative meanings?

2 What do you think news reporting was like when it first started?

Vocabulary Preview

A **Match the words with their definitions by writing the correct letters in the blanks.**

1 profession _____ a. shocking; ridiculous

2 sensational _____ b. intended to produce a strong reaction

3 headline _____ c. to hide one's identity to try to discover something

4 scandal _____ d. a job that requires special knowledge or training

5 outrageous _____ e. the act of being dishonest or doing something illegal

6 battleship _____ f. to make changes that improve someone or something

7 blame _____ g. an action that causes harm to a person's reputation

8 corruption _____ h. a large naval ship with thick armor and heavy weapons

9 reform (v.) _____ i. to say that someone is responsible for doing something bad

10 go undercover _____ j. the large type on a newspaper announcing the most important news

B **Choose the words that have similar (*sim.*) or opposite (*opp.*) meanings from the box.**

opponent	reject	especially

1 particularly _____ *sim.*

2 supporter _____ *opp.*

3 refuse _____ *sim.*

Background Knowledge

In the 1800s, newspapers had a huge influence on American society. They were the only source of news for most people. In order to sell more papers, newspapers printed stories that were guaranteed to shock people. These stories were entertaining to read, but they did not always contain the truth.

Yellow Journalism and Muckraking

Q

What is each paragraph mainly about?

P1 The (importance / failure) of journalism in the 1700s and 1800s

Journalism was important to the United States even before it became a country. During the 1700s and 1800s, most people got their news by reading newspapers and magazines. The written word was particularly important then since there was no radio or TV. However, the **profession**
5 went through various changes. In the late 1800s, two new terms began to be connected to journalism. They were yellow journalism and *muckraking.

P2 How newspapers tried to _____ readers

At the end of the nineteenth century, the newspaper industry was very competitive. Most big cities had two or more newspapers. They were always trying to attract more readers. So many of them began printing
10 stories with **sensational headlines**. The stories were often about crimes and **scandals**, yet there was usually little truth to them. This practice came to be known as yellow journalism.

P3 Which newspapers (opposed / supported) yellow journalism and how they led the U.S. to war

Two of the biggest supporters of yellow journalism were Joseph Pulitzer's *New York World* and William Randolph Hearst's *New York*
15 *Journal*. Every day, they printed more and more **outrageous** headlines. Then, the *U.S.S. Maine*, a **battleship**, exploded in Havana, Cuba. The two papers **blamed** Spain. Their headlines and stories helped encourage the American people to get the U.S. government to
20 declare war on Spain. This resulted in the Spanish-American War.

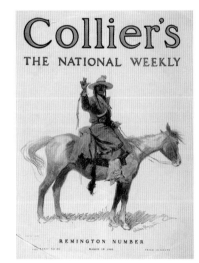

P4 (What / Why) muckrakers did and who they wrote about

Not all journalists reported sensational stories though. Others tried to find scandals and **corruption** in society. These
25 journalists, called muckrakers, mostly wrote about politicians and business

leaders. They were trying to find the truth to **reform** society through their muckraking. Most newspapers refused to print their stories, so they turned to magazines such as *McClure's* and *Collier's*.

Muckrakers published stories on the oil, coal mining, and meat-packing industries. Some even **went undercover** to work in these industries. Then, they could expose the problems from the inside. Thanks to them, there were many positive reforms made in American society. Words 300

30 🄿🄴 What the results of the stories by _____ were

*muckrake: to search for corruption or scandals, especially in politics

i The Spanish-American War largely started because of the actions of newspapers encouraging war. It started in 1898, and the American battle cry was, "Remember the *Maine*." When it ended, Cuba gained its independence, and the United States got Puerto Rico, Guam, and the Philippines from Spain.

 Check the main idea of the passage.

   a. Yellow journalism was the cause of the decline of the newspaper industry.

   b. Muckrakers in the United States wrote stories about various scandals.

   c. Newspapers were the best way Americans could get news in the 1800s.

   d. Journalism in the late 1800s was filled with yellow journalism and muckraking.

Reading Comprehension

1 In paragraph 1, all of the following questions are answered EXCEPT:

   a. What sources of news did people rely on in the 1700s and 1800s?

   b. Why was the written word so important to people in the past?

   c. What were the names of some newspapers in the 1700s and 1800s?

   d. What new terms in journalism were created in the late 1800s?

2 According to paragraph 2, which of the following is true about yellow journalism?

   a. It appeared in newspapers in every big city.

   b. It featured stories that were not completely true.

   c. It resulted from the fierce competition between readers.

   d. It referred only to sensational headlines in newspapers.

3 Why does the author mention the *U.S.S. Maine*?

   a. To mention that Joseph Pulitzer once sailed on it

   b. To call it the most powerful battleship in the world

   c. To explain its role in starting the Spanish-American War

   d. To note that an article about it appeared in the *New York Journal*

4 The word They in the passage refers to

   a. Scandals and corruption   b. These journalists

   c. Politicians   d. Business leaders

5 In paragraphs 4 and 5, which of the following is NOT mentioned about muckrakers?

   a. What kinds of problems they tried to find in society

   b. How many reforms they were responsible for

   c. Which magazines they were published in

   d. Which industries they often wrote about

6 Who were the two biggest supporters of yellow journalism?

   They were _____.

7 Who did the muckrakers mostly write about?

   _____

98

Organizing the Passage

Complete the organizer with the phrases in the box.

Yellow Journalism and Muckraking

Journalism	• It was important in the United States in ❶_____ because it was people's main source of news. • The newspaper industry was ❷_____ in the late 1800s.
Yellow Journalism	• Newspapers published stories that had ❸_____ and that had little truth. • Joseph Pulitzer's *New York World* and William Randolph Hearst's *New York Journal* were ❹_____ of it. • They helped the United States get involved in the Spanish-American War.
Muckraking	• Some muckrakers tried to find ❺_____ in society. • They often wrote about politicians and business leaders. • They wanted to ❻_____ through their muckraking.

scandals and corruption   very competitive   reform society
the 1700s and 1800s   big supporters   sensational headlines

Summarizing the Passage

Use the phrases in the box to complete the summary.

desire war   went undercover
published in magazines   yellow journalism   had little truth

In the United States in the 1700s and 1800s, many people got their news from newspapers. In the late 1800s, ❶_____ started. It featured sensational headlines and stories that ❷_____. The newspapers of Joseph Pulitzer and William Randolph Hearst supported yellow journalism. They even got the American people to ❸_____ against Spain. Other journalists were muckrakers. They wrote about scandals and corruption in society. They wanted to reform society. Their stories were often ❹_____. Some muckrakers ❺_____ to learn about problems in certain industries.

Unit 14
Citizen Journalists

Think about the Topic

1 Who are citizen journalists?

2 How can a person become a journalist?

Vocabulary Preview

A **Match the words with their definitions by writing the correct letters in the blanks.**

1 publication _____ a. to help

2 mass media _____ b. to say or write bad things about

3 print _____ c. an instance of visiting a website

4 assist _____ d. not to believe someone or something

5 audience _____ e. anything that is published in written form

6 hit _____ f. unfairly preferring someone over another

7 disaster _____ g. people who read something or watch an event

8 distrust _____ h. a terrible event, often where people are hurt or die

9 biased _____ i. something printed such as a book, magazine, or newspaper

10 criticize _____ j. any type of communication, such as a newspaper or TV, that reaches a large number of people

B **Choose the words that have similar (*sim.*) or opposite (*opp.*) meanings from the box.**

professional	machine	connect

1 device _____ *sim.*

2 link _____ *sim.*

3 amateur _____ *opp.*

Background Knowledge

Thanks to the Internet and improved communication methods, anyone can be a journalist. The term citizen journalist started after the Southeast Asian tsunami in 2004. Many people took photos and videos of affected areas and put them online. Today, citizen journalists report the news on blogs, personal webpages, and even YouTube.

Citizen Journalists

Q

What is each paragraph mainly about?

P1 (How / Where) journalism has changed since the 1900s

In the 1900s, nearly all journalism was done by professionals. They were paid to write for newspapers, magazines, and other types of **publications**. This began to _____ at the end of the century. Thanks to modern technology, regular people now engage in what is called citizen
5 journalism.

P2 The importance of modern _____ for citizen journalists

Before the creation of the World Wide Web, the only way to spread **mass media** was through **print**. But these days, citizen journalists are able to publish their stories on the Internet. They also use modern technology to **assist** them. ❶ They utilize cellphones, digital cameras, and laptop
10 computers. ❷ These devices let them produce written, video, and audio stories. ❸ They often do this while events are still going on. ❹

P3 How citizen journalists (watch / report) the news

Many citizen journalists have blogs. Most blogs have small **audiences**, yet others get thousands of **hits** a day. If a news report on a blog is linked by a popular website, it can get millions of hits. Other citizen journalists
15 upload videos onto the Internet. They use YouTube, BitChute, and other video-hosting websites to do that.

P4 What kinds of (people / events) citizen journalists report on

Some people are citizen journalists full time. Others are citizen journalists for a single day. They see an event and report on it, often by using Facebook or Twitter. Common
20 events they report on are crimes, **disasters**, wars, and politics. Citizen journalists are often the first to report on breaking news. So the reports they make and the videos they shoot are valuable.
25

Many young people get their news from the Internet. They **distrust** mass media due to the **biased** reporting of many journalists. So young people tend to trust citizen journalists more. Professional journalists, on the other hand, often **criticize** citizen journalists. They call them biased amateurs. They also say their reporting is of low quality. Still, citizen journalism is here to stay. And it will likely be even more popular in the future. Words 316

P5 How _____ journalists and citizen journalists feel about each other

30

 Check the main point of the passage.

a. Professional journalists are biased and rely on fake news.

b. There are many ways that people can publish the news nowadays.

c. Regular people can report on news events thanks to modern technology.

d. Some professionals have started to report the news on blogs and webpages.

i In recent years, citizen journalists have broken many important news stories. For instance, in 2011, the raid that killed Osama bin Laden was reported by a citizen journalist one day before the U.S. government announced it.

Reading Comprehension

1 What is the best choice for the blank?

   a. change

   b. develop

   c. be popular

   d. happen rarely

2 Where would the following sentence best fit in paragraph 2?

They can then upload their news reports to the Internet.

   a. ❶   b. ❷   c. ❸   d. ❹

3 According to paragraph 3, which of the following is NOT true about blogs?

   a. Some of them can get lots of hits.

   b. Popular websites may link to them.

   c. Citizen journalists often use them.

   d. They are expensive to operate.

4 The word shoot in the passage is closest in meaning to

   a. conduct   b. record   c. explode   d. fire

5 Which of the following CANNOT be inferred about citizen journalists?

   a. They are good at using the Internet.

   b. More people will visit their websites.

   c. They can report some news faster than professionals.

   d. The number of full-time citizen journalists is increasing.

6 What do citizen journalists report on?

   They report on _____.

7 Why do young people distrust mass media?

   _____

Organizing the Passage

Complete the organizer with the phrases in the box.

Citizen Journalists

How Modern Technology Affects Journalism	• The World Wide Web allows citizen journalists to ❶_____ on the Internet. • They produce ❷_____ stories by using digital devices.
How They Report the News	• Many of them use blogs, which can get ❸_____ if popular websites link to them. • They use websites such as YouTube and BitChute to upload videos. • They may use Facebook or Twitter to report on ❹_____, and politics.
What People Think about Them	• ❺_____ them more than they trust professional journalists because they are biased. • Professional journalists say that citizen journalists are biased and their reporting is ❻_____.

publish their stories	crimes, disasters, wars	low in quality
young people trust	written, video, and audio	millions of hits

Summarizing the Passage

Use the phrases in the box to complete the summary.

work full time	publish stories
Facebook or Twitter	distrust mass media	the World Wide Web

Most journalism was done by professionals in the 1900s, but this is changing. Thanks to

❶_____, there are now citizen journalists. Many of them use blogs to

❷_____, and others upload videos onto the Internet. Some citizen journalists

❸_____, but others only work for a day. They may use ❹_____

to report on breaking news stories. Young people often ❺_____ but trust citizen

journalists. However, professional journalists criticize citizen journalists and say their reporting

is low in quality.

Chapter 8

Astronomy

Astronomy refers to the study of the stars, planets, and everything else in the universe. Astronomers use telescopes and other high-tech instruments to examine the objects in the night sky to learn more about them.

Water in the Solar System

Think about the Topic

1 Where in the solar system do you think there is water?

2 Why is it important to find water in the solar system?

Vocabulary Preview

A **Match the words with their definitions by writing the correct letters in the blanks.**

1 solar system _____ a. to guess; to suppose

2 matter _____ b. steam; water in its gaseous form

3 abundance _____ c. the length, area, or amount of something

4 asteroid _____ d. more than enough in supply or amount

5 water vapor _____ e. the sun and all the objects that move around it

6 satellite _____ f. a small, rocky planet that moves around the sun

7 estimate _____ g. a flight by a spacecraft to do something specific

8 telescope _____ h. a moon; an object that moves around a planet

9 mission _____ i. the material that everything in the universe is made of

10 extent _____ j. an object used to look at distant objects to make them appear larger

B **Choose the words that have similar** (*sim.*) **or opposite** (*opp.*) **meanings from the box.**

absent	shortage	capacity

1 abundance _____ *opp.*

2 volume _____ *sim.*

3 present (*a.*) _____ *opp.*

Background Knowledge

Life on Earth is only possible because of the existence of water. In the future, humans may establish colonies on the moon, planets such as Mars, or satellites such as Europa or Io. Colonies would need large amounts of water to survive. Astronomers hope to find water on these places and in other locations in the solar system. That will make it easier for people to establish colonies.

Water in the Solar System

Q

What is each paragraph mainly about?

P1 Where in the _____ there is water

P2 Where water on (Mars / Pluto) can be found

P3 Which (planets / satellites) may have water beneath their surfaces

Water can be found throughout the **solar system** in a wide variety of places. It exists in all three states of **matter**: solid, liquid, and gas. In addition to being on the Earth in **abundance**, there is water on planets, moons, and **asteroids** in the solar system. Astronomers find this to be of
5 great interest since water is needed for life to exist.

Of the eight major planets, water exists on the surface of both Earth and Mars. On Mars, it is mainly in the form of ice. A small amount exists in the atmosphere as **water vapor** though. Most of Mars's frozen water is located at its northern and southern poles in the form of large ice caps.
10 Astronomers also believe—but are not sure—that Pluto and Ceres, two dwarf planets, have water.

Many planetary **satellites** have water. ❶ Europa, a moon of Jupiter, has a large liquid water ocean beneath its surface. ❷ It is **estimated** to contain twice the volume of all the water on the Earth. ❸ Ganymede, another of
15 Jupiter's moons, has an even larger ocean of liquid water under its surface. ❹ Some estimate it contains around thirty-five times more water than the Earth.

▶ Jupiter and its moons

▲ Frozen water on Mars

Water can be found on many asteroids, primarily in the form of ice, too. It exists as ice crystals in the rings of the gas giant planets. They are Saturn, Jupiter, Uranus, and Neptune. Astronomers also think that water is present 20 in the interiors of the gas giants.

P4 Where water exists in the _____

Finding water outside the Earth has not been an easy task. Most of the information collected so far has come from long-range **telescopes**. However, this may change soon. Both NASA and the European Space Agency are planning **missions** to Europa. They will map the moon's surface 25 and determine the **extent** of its water resources. Words 311

P5 (Why / How) astronomers find water outside the Earth

 Check what the passage is mainly about.

a. The reasons that astronomers are looking for water on planets

b. The moons in the solar system known to have liquid water

c. The amount of water the planets in the solar system have

d. The places in the solar system where there is water

i A dwarf planet is a large, rocky mass that moves around the sun and is not a moon. However, it is too small for it to be called a planet. There are five dwarf planets in the solar system. They are Pluto, Ceres, Eris, Makemake, and Haumea.

Reading Comprehension

1 In paragraph 2, all of the following questions are answered EXCEPT:

   a. Which major planets have water?

   b. Which form of water exists at the poles of Mars?

   c. Which dwarf planets are thought to have water?

   d. Why do scientists think there is water on dwarf planets?

2 Where would the following sentence best fit in paragraph 3?

It may be the largest water source in the entire solar system.

   a. ❶   b. ❷   c. ❸   d. ❹

3 The word primarily in the passage is closest in meaning to

   a. originally   b. only   c. mainly   d. considerably

4 Which of the following is NOT true according to the passage?

   a. Mars and dwarf planets have water only in the form of ice.

   b. There is water in the rings of Saturn and Uranus.

   c. Water exists as a gas in some places in the solar system.

   d. There are oceans of liquid water beneath Jupiter's moons.

5 According to paragraph 5, which of the following is true about Europa?

   a. NASA has already sent a satellite there.

   b. Some missions will be sent to explore it.

   c. A long-range telescope has mapped its surface.

   d. It is known to have some huge underground lakes.

6 How much water may be in the ocean on Ganymede?

   Astronomers estimate it contains _____.

7 Where is most of Mars's frozen water located?

   _____

Organizing the Passage

Complete the organizer with the phrases in the box.

	Water in the Solar System
Earth and Mars	• Water is located ❶_____ of both Earth and Mars. • There is water vapor on Mars, and its northern and southern poles also have ice caps.
Jupiter's Moons	• Europa has an ocean under its surface that has ❷_____ on the Earth. • Ganymede may have thirty-five times the amount of the Earth's water in ❸_____.
Asteroids and Gas Giants	• There is water ❹_____ on many asteroids. • The gas giants Jupiter, Saturn, Uranus, and Neptune have ice crystals in their rings. • The gas giants may have water ❺_____.
Finding Water	• Astronomers use long-range telescopes to search for water. • NASA and the European Space Agency will ❻_____ to look for water.

in their interiors	twice the water	in the form of ice
send satellites to Europa	on the surface	its underground ocean

Summarizing the Passage

The first sentence of a short summary is provided below. Complete the summary by choosing THREE answer choices that express the most important ideas.

> Water exists in a wide number of places in the solar system.

1 Astronomers believe that every planet in the solar system has liquid water on it.

2 Water is known to exist on the surface of the Earth and is in its gaseous and frozen forms on Mars.

3 The water that can be found throughout the solar system will likely be used by humans one day.

4 Planetary satellites such as two moons of Jupiter are believed to have very large oceans beneath their surfaces.

5 Some believe that the gas giants not only have ice in their rings but also have water in their interiors.

Unit 16

Galaxies and Their Formation

Think about the Topic

1 What is the name of the galaxy our solar system is in?

2 How many stars do you think galaxies have?

Vocabulary Preview

A **Match the words with their definitions by writing the correct letters in the blanks.**

1 universe   _____   a. to make up

2 comprise   _____   b. very large and heavy

3 massive   _____   c. lacking an even shape

4 primary   _____   d. main; most important

5 spiral   _____   e. circling around a central point

6 elliptical   _____   f. to move around in a circle

7 irregular   _____   g. everything that exists in space

8 expand   _____   h. very tiny pieces of dirt or other objects

9 dust   _____   i. to become larger or greater in size or amount

10 rotate   _____   j. rounded in shape similar to a fattened circle

B **Choose the words that have similar** (*sim.*) **or opposite** (*opp.*) **meanings from the box.**

break down	circle	enormous

1 orbit   _____ *sim.*

2 tiny   _____ *opp.*

3 collapse   _____ *sim.*

Background Knowledge

Astronomers believe that the universe was created around fourteen billion years ago. That was when the Big Bang occurred. Soon afterward, galaxies made of stars began to form. There are billions of galaxies in the universe, and most of them have billions of stars. In fact, nobody is sure how many stars there are in the universe.

Galaxies and Their Formation

Q

What is each paragraph mainly about?

P1 Who came up with the theory that (galaxies / universes) exist

P2 (Where / What) a galaxy is

P3 The four _____ types of galaxies and their characteristics

In the past, people believed that all the stars in the **universe** were located in a single group. Then, in the 1900s, Thomas Wright came up with a theory. He thought there were many large groups of stars. This idea was soon proved correct, and that was when the term galaxy started to be used.

5　A galaxy is an enormous group of stars and the objects that orbit them. Most galaxies are **comprised** of billions of stars. They circle around a center that contains a **massive** black hole. The Milky Way Galaxy, which is where Earth is located, has about 300 billion stars in it.

Not all galaxies look alike. Astronomers have identified four **primary**
10　types of galaxies: **spiral**, barred spiral, **elliptical**, and **irregular** galaxies. Spiral galaxies have several long arms that spiral around the center. Typically, young stars are in the spirals while older ones are closer to the center. Barred spiral galaxies have a bar in the middle and spiral arms coming off their ends. The sun is found in one of the spiral arms of the
15　Milky Way. Elliptical galaxies have large numbers of stars grouped together

▲ An elliptical galaxy

▲ A barred spiral galaxy

▲ A spiral galaxy

to form an elliptical disk. Finally, irregular galaxies have a variety of shapes. They are thought to be created when two galaxies collide with each other.

Galaxies started being created after the formation of the universe. According to the Big Bang Theory, the universe formed around fourteen billion years ago. All the matter in the universe was contained in a tiny point that suddenly started to **expand** rapidly. After the Big Bang occurred, galaxies started to form. Astronomers think that clouds of hydrogen, helium, and **dust** gathered. Then, the force of gravity caused these clouds to form stars. When the clouds collapsed due to gravity, they formed **rotating** disks. These disks attracted more gas and dust, so more stars formed. Over time, enough stars formed to create galaxies. Words 318

P4 How galaxies may have _____

20

25

 Check what the passage is mainly about.

   a. What galaxies are and how they were created

   b. What kinds of stars can be found within galaxies

   c. How the Big Bang created the entire universe

   d. How the Milky Way and all of its stars formed

i The Milky Way is a barred spiral galaxy. It is a medium-sized galaxy. Earth's solar system is located in one of the spiral arms of the Milky Way. On dark nights, it is possible to see part of the Milky Way in the night sky.

Reading Comprehension

1 The word it in the passage refers to

   a. a center

   b. a massive black hole

   c. the Milky Way Galaxy

   d. Earth

2 The word spiral in the passage is closest in meaning to

   a. circle   b. shape   c. attract   d. group

3 In paragraph 3, all of the following questions are answered EXCEPT:

   a. What are the four main types of galaxies?

   b. Which type of galaxy is the most common?

   c. Where are young stars located in spiral galaxies?

   d. How do astronomers think irregular galaxies formed?

4 Why does the author mention the Big Bang Theory?

   a. To mention what caused it to happen

   b. To claim that it has been proved incorrect

   c. To name the astronomer who thought of it

   d. To explain how the universe was created

5 According to the passage, which of following CANNOT be inferred about galaxies?

   a. Some galaxies collide with one another.

   b. Nobody is sure exactly how they formed.

   c. They have more black holes than they do stars.

   d. They formed after the creation of the universe.

6 What is at the center of most galaxies?

   At the center of most galaxies is _____.

7 What does a barred spiral galaxy look like?

   _____

Organizing the Passage

Complete the organizer with the phrases in the box.

Galaxies and Their Formation

What Galaxies Are	• They are enormous ❶_____ and the objects that orbit them. • They have a massive black hole at their center.
The Four Types of Galaxies	• ❷_____ have several long arms that spiral around the center. • Barred spiral galaxies have a bar in the middle and spiral arms ❸_____. • Elliptical galaxies have stars that combine to form an elliptical disk. • ❹_____ have many different shapes.
The Big Bang Theory and the Formation of Galaxies	• The universe started around ❺_____ years ago according to the Big Bang Theory. • Clouds of hydrogen, helium, and dust gathered. • Gravity caused the clouds to form stars and rotating disks. • ❻_____ in rotating disk and created galaxies.

group of stars	fourteen billion	enough stars formed
coming off their ends	irregular galaxies	spiral galaxies

Summarizing the Passage

Use the phrases in the box to complete the summary.

galaxies formed	different shapes	
clouds of hydrogen	billions of stars	primary types

Galaxies are huge groups of stars. Many contain ❶_____, and most of them have a massive black hole in their center. There are four ❷_____ of galaxies. Spiral galaxies and barred spiral galaxies both have arms. Elliptical galaxies have somewhat circular shapes while irregular galaxies have many ❸_____. Galaxies did not form until after the Big Bang created the universe. There were ❹_____, helium, and dust that gathered and made stars. Then, rotating disks formed, and that made more stars form. When enough stars were created, ❺_____.

TOEFL
Practice Test

The Benefits and Drawbacks of Dams

Dams are obstructions that are placed across flowing water such as rivers and streams. The result is that lakes are created behind them. The flow of water downriver or downstream is slowed, too. Dams provide a large number of benefits but also have some drawbacks.

In modern times, the main advantage of dams is that they are used to provide electricity. ■ The electricity created from them is called hydroelectric power. ■ Basically, the running water permitted to pass through dams makes turbines spin, which, in turn, creates electricity that is cheap, clean, and renewable. ■ These days, hydroelectric power accounts for nearly twenty percent of the world's power needs. ■

The reservoirs created by dams also provide benefits to people. The water in them is used to supply residences with drinking water. Farmers also use the water to irrigate their fields. People often engage in various water activities on the reservoirs. Among them are fishing, boating, and swimming.

There are downsides to dams though. One is that constructing them can be time consuming and expensive. Construction is labor intensive and must be precise, or the dam could have future problems. For instance, the Three Gorges Dam in China is a huge dam across the Yangtze River. Today, it has visible cracks. If water breaks through it, it could have disastrous consequences for people living downriver.

Dams also obstruct the flow of water, which can harm the ecosystems of rivers and streams. Some animals require free-flowing water to survive. Dams ensure that they no longer have that. In addition, dams prevent valuable *silt from going downriver. This is true of the Aswan Dam across the Nile River. Farmers in Egypt used to plant crops in the silt carried by the river during annual floods, but they can no longer do that. Additionally, the reservoirs dams create flood the land. In some cases, forests, fields, and even towns and villages have been covered by water.

*silt: dirt and sand that are carried by running water such as rivers and streams

---

1   **Where would the following sentence best fit in paragraph 2?**

As a result, people who use power from dams have low electric bills.

2   **In paragraph 3, all of the following questions are answered EXCEPT:**

Ⓐ How do residences use the water in reservoirs?

Ⓑ What activities do people do on reservoirs made by dams?

Ⓒ What use do farmers have for reservoirs made by dams?

Ⓓ How is the water collected in reservoirs moved to fields?

3   **In paragraph 4, the author uses "the Three Gorges Dam" as an example of**

Ⓐ one of the largest dams ever made

Ⓑ a dam that has some construction problems

Ⓒ the last dam built over the Yangtze River

Ⓓ an example of a dam that cost a lot to build

4   **The word "obstruct" in the passage is closest in meaning to**

Ⓐ permit

Ⓑ block

Ⓒ arrange

Ⓓ avoid

5   **In paragraph 5, the author's description of the Aswan Dam mentions which of the following?**

Ⓐ How large the reservoir it created is

Ⓑ How it has endangered some animals

Ⓒ How it is causing harm to some Egyptians

Ⓓ How it changed the course of the Nile River

6   **An introductory sentence for a brief summary of the passage is provided below. Complete the summary by selecting the THREE answer choices that express the most important ideas of the passage.**

> Dams have both advantages and disadvantages.

❶ Dams can have negative effects on the ecosystems of the areas they are in.

❷ The hydroelectric power created by dams creates clean and cheap electricity.

❸ The Aswan Dam and the Three Gorges Dam are two of the world's biggest dams.

❹ People have been making dams across rivers and streams for thousands of years.

❺ The water in the reservoirs formed by dams can be used for people and farming.

Symbiosis

All creatures interact with one another. In some cases, their interactions are important to the survival of one or both participants. This is known as symbiosis. There are three major types of symbiotic relationships: mutualism, commensalism, and parasitism.

Mutualism is a form of symbiosis in which both organisms involved benefit while neither is harmed. One example is the relationship between remoras and sharks. Remoras are sucker fish that attach themselves to the bodies of sharks. They get a free ride and eat leftover food after the sharks feed. Remoras also eat parasites on sharks' bodies, so the sharks gain by having harmful animals removed. ■ In the plant world, many flowers attract bees, wasps, and other insects that consume the nectar flowers produce. ■ They then spread pollen to other flowers. ■ This lets flowers be pollinated. ■ They can then produce fruit and later reproduce.

In commensalism, only one organism benefits. However, no harm is done to either. The bird called the cattle egret depends upon cows for food. As cows move through fields, they cause insects to move around and to fly away. The egrets catch the insects and consume them. In this relationship, the egrets benefit. And nothing harmful happens to the cows.

Parasitism results in harm—and sometimes death—to one party involved while the other organism benefits. Fleas are parasites that live on the bodies of dogs. They bite dogs and consume their blood, which makes the dogs develop rashes and itchy bodies. Aphids are insects that eat the sap of certain plants. This weakens and even kills the plants. The cuckoo bird lays its eggs in the nests of other birds to avoid raising its own young. Baby cuckoos are large birds, so they consume more resources. The other baby birds are therefore harmed.

All three types of symbiosis that exist are common around the world. In many cases, animals would not survive without engaging in these relationships.

---

1   **According to paragraph 2, remoras benefit because**

   Ⓐ sharks do not try to hunt and kill them

   Ⓑ they can save energy by not having to hunt

   Ⓒ they can eat the food that sharks leave behind

   Ⓓ the parasites on their bodies are eaten by sharks

2   **Where would the following sentence best fit in paragraph 2?**

   In a similar manner, some birds eat food stuck in the teeth of crocodiles, which benefits both animals.

3 The word "**them**" in the passage refers to

(A) cows   (B) fields   (C) the egrets   (D) the insects

4 Which of the sentences below best expresses the essential information in the highlighted sentence in the passage? *Incorrect* answer choices change the meaning in important ways or leave out essential information.

Parasitism results in harm—and sometimes death—to one party involved while the other organism benefits.

(A) Parasitism always results in the death of one organism.

(B) In parasitism, one organism gains while the other is hurt.

(C) Two parties must be involved for parasitism to occur.

(D) It is possible for some parasites to benefit other organisms.

5 In paragraph 4, the author uses "**The cuckoo bird**" as an example of

(A) a parasite that harms other creatures

(B) an animal that engages in mutualism

(C) the most common type of symbiosis

(D) a bird that relies on parasitism to raise its young

6 Select the appropriate statements from the answer choices and match them to type of symbiosis to which they relate. Two of the answer choices will NOT be used.

STATEMENTS	TYPE OF SYMBIOSIS
1 Can result in one organism killing the other	**Mutualism** (Select 3)
2 Takes place when aphids consume the sap of some trees	•
3 Does not result in either organism suffering any harm while both benefit	• •
4 Is the most common form of symbiosis in the animal world	**Commensalism** (Select 2)
5 Can only take place between animals and plants	•
6 Benefits one organism while not having a negative effect on the other	•
7 Happens when remoras eat parasites on sharks' bodies	**Parasitism** (Select 2)
8 Is the type of relationship egrets have with cows	•
9 Is behavior that enables many flowers to get pollinated	•

Zoning Laws in Urban Areas

First-time homeowners often express one major concern before signing a contract for a new home. They are worried about what buildings will be erected in their new neighborhood. For instance, young families have no interest in buying a house on a street where a factory will be built. Fortunately for them, zoning laws exist.

Zoning laws are made by governments. They restrict the use of land for certain purposes. The main goal of zoning is to guarantee that new buildings do not interfere with existing ones. This lets residential areas remain free of industries. Zoning laws also help preserve historic areas. As an example, they might forbid certain old buildings with historical value from being torn down. Finally, zoning laws may put restrictions on the sizes of buildings, the materials used for them, and their specific placements.

The origins of zoning go back thousands of years. In ancient times, cities had defensive walls. These protected residents against invaders. The walls also served as zoning borders. Noisy and smelly activities were done outside the walls. That was also where the poor lived and worked. Some cities had multiple walls around them. Unsanitary and dangerous activities were done between them. That was where butchers worked and waste disposal was done. Inside the walls were civic and religious areas as well as residences.

Today, there are four urban zones: residential, mixed residential and commercial, commercial, and spatial. Residential areas are for homes. Commercial areas have stores and restaurants. Power plants, airports, and sports stadiums are in spatial zones. Only buildings meant for a zone's purpose can be built in that area. Thus no one can build a house in a commercial zone. Shopping malls may also not be made in residential areas.

Zoning enables cities to develop as they were planned. It creates a safe environment for people and businesses. And it makes cities look better and be cleaner.

1   **In paragraphs 1 and 2, the author implies that zoning laws**

   Ⓐ benefit people who purchase homes

   Ⓑ have been used by cities only recently

   Ⓒ may cause economic problems for cities

   Ⓓ can be easily changed by city leaders

2 **According to paragraph 2, zoning laws are used to**

Ⓐ let some buildings be made bigger than other ones

Ⓑ stop new buildings from making problems for existing ones

Ⓒ allow cities to develop the way their founders intended

Ⓓ keep people living only in certain neighborhoods in cities

3 **The word "them" in the passage refers to**

Ⓐ noisy and smelly activities

Ⓑ the poor

Ⓒ some cities

Ⓓ multiple walls

4 **The word "Unsanitary" in the passage is closest in meaning to**

Ⓐ unknown

Ⓑ unclean

Ⓒ unspoken

Ⓓ uneventful

5 **In paragraph 4, why does the author mention "Power plants, airports, and sports stadiums"?**

Ⓐ To prove that zoning laws are effective

Ⓑ To emphasize that they belong in commercial zones

Ⓒ To claim that some houses may be built by them

Ⓓ To show which places can go into a certain zone

6 **An introductory sentence for a brief summary of the passage is provided below. Complete the summary by selecting the THREE answer choices that express the most important ideas of the passage.**

Zoning laws provide a number of benefits by creating distinct areas in cities.

❶ New homeowners are often not aware of the zoning laws in their cities.

❷ Zoning laws have separated areas of cities from one another for thousands of years.

❸ Zoning laws make sure that land in cities is used for its original intentions.

❹ Some zones are for people to live in whereas others are for businesses and factories.

❺ Airports, sports stadiums, and religious areas are usually in their own special zones.

The Secret Ballot

People have been voting in elections since the time of ancient Greece more than 2,000 years ago. There are several ways to vote. There are voice votes, where people announce who they are voting for. Sometimes people merely raise their hands to vote. There are also paper ballots that people mark their selections on and modern electronic voting machines.

In most cases today, the selections people make are done by secret ballot. This means nobody else knows who a person voted for. The secret ballot has several benefits. One is that it reduces voter intimidation. This happens when people feel like they must vote for a candidate, or something bad will happen to them. It further reduces voter suppression. In that case, fewer people vote in elections since they do not want their choices to be announced in public.

In ancient Greece, people often voted in public. But some votes were done by secret ballot. These were usually sensitive matters. These included deciding on the life or death of an individual or whether or not to exile a person. In the second century B.C., the Roman Republic introduced a series of laws. They called for the secret ballot in almost all elections. This resulted in public participation in voting to increase.

In recent centuries, there were attempts by various individuals and governments to get rid of the secret ballot. These were mostly opposed by regular people. In the United States during the 1800s, states slowly began to do away with oral ballots. By the year 1892, only secret ballots were used in the country. England, Australia, and New Zealand also passed laws regarding the secret ballot during the 1800s. As for France, it guaranteed the secret ballot in the early 1900s.

Most people today are unfamiliar with anything other than the secret ballot. However, in spite of its many benefits, it was not universal until recent times.

1　**According to paragraph 1, which of the following is NOT true about how people can vote?**

Ⓐ They can say who they are voting for out loud.

Ⓑ They can make their selections on paper.

Ⓒ They can submit their ballots through the mail.

Ⓓ They can put their hands up in the air to vote.

2   The word "intimidation" in the passage is closest in meaning to

Ⓐ turnout

Ⓑ knowledge

Ⓒ arguing

Ⓓ bullying

3   The author discusses "the Roman Republic" in paragraph 3 in order to

Ⓐ compare its election rules with those of Greece

Ⓑ give an example of a place where no elections were held

Ⓒ describe how it officially began to use the secret ballot

Ⓓ prove it was the first place to use the secret ballot

4   The word "These" in the passage refers to

Ⓐ Recent centuries

Ⓑ Attempts

Ⓒ Various individuals

Ⓓ Governments

5   In paragraph 4, the author's description of the secret ballot mentions which of the following?

Ⓐ Which countries passed laws about it in the 1800s

Ⓑ How regular people opposed efforts against it

Ⓒ Why some governments tried to get rid of it

Ⓓ What countries do not require it in their elections

6   An introductory sentence for a brief summary of the passage is provided below. Complete the summary by selecting the THREE answer choices that express the most important ideas of the passage.

> The secret ballot has many advantages, and people have been using it for centuries.

❶ Many countries began to use the secret ballot in the 1800s.

❷ There are many countries around the world that do not use the secret ballot.

❸ The ancient Greeks and Romans used the secret ballot to vote on certain issues.

❹ More people vote, and there is less voter intimidation and suppression thanks to it.

❺ Some people vote with paper ballots, but others use voting machines these days.

MEMO

MEMO

MEMO

Building Background Knowledge for Academic Subjects

Fundamental Reading

Workbook

PLUS **2**

DARAKWON

Building Background Knowledge for Academic Subjects

Fundamental Reading

Michael A. Putlack
Stephen Poirier
Tony Covello

Workbook

PLUS 2

DARAKWON

Unit 1 **Sustainable Architecture**

Vocabulary

A **Read the sentences and choose the best words for the blanks.**

1 Since a sponge can **absorb** liquids, I will use one to _____ the mess on the floor.

   a. soak up   b. throw away   c. sweep up   d. vacuum

2 The **premise** she suggested is interesting, but Greg has another _____.

   a. task   b. idea   c. question   d. problem

3 The Western **Hemisphere** is the _____ of the Earth that includes North and South America.

   a. half   b. ecosystem   c. environment   d. continent

B **Choose the words from the box to complete the sentences.**

insulation	eliminate	evergreen trees	internal	multistory

1 She lives on the top floor of a _____ building.

2 They planted some _____ on one side of the house.

3 The building needs a lot of _____ to keep it warm in winter.

4 The materials in the building will _____ the need to use air conditioning.

5 The _____ temperature of the building is higher than the outside temperature.

Translation

C **Read the sentences and translate them into your language.**

1 The basic premise of it is to make housing which reduces energy usage.

  → _____

2 These windows have two pieces of glass with air between them.

  → _____

3 One method architects use is to make homes that need less internal heating and cooling.

  → _____

Paraphrasing

D **Paraphrase the sentences from the passage with the words and phrases in the box.**

| stop | protects | is bad for | soak up the sun's rays |
| spend less | lots of electricity | from getting hot |

1 Architects design large windows facing the sun, where they can absorb sunlight.

→ Architects make big windows that face the sun in order to _____.

2 It can help the environment and save people money on energy costs.

→ It _____ the environment and lets people _____ on electricity.

3 In summer, the leaves of these trees block sunlight, which keeps homes cool.

→ In summer, the leaves of the trees _____ sunlight from getting through and keep homes _____.

4 Heating and cooling homes requires a great amount of energy, which can harm the environment.

→ Heating and cooling houses uses _____, which _____ the environment.

Listening

E **Listen to the summary and fill in the blanks.**

Many ❶ _____ design homes based on sustainable architecture, so they use
❷ _____ energy and cause less harm to the environment. They make homes
that need less internal ❸ _____ and cooling. Architects use windows
❹ _____ the sun to make homes ❺ _____. They also design one-story
buildings, which let heat easily ❻ _____ through the roofs. Inside homes,
❼ _____ can keep buildings cool in summer and warm in winter. Gas-insulated
windows can insulate homes, too. ❽ _____ trees north of homes can block the
wind in cold climates. Deciduous trees can ❾ _____ sunlight in summer and let
light ❿ _____ homes in winter.

Unit 2 Shipping Container Homes

Vocabulary

A **Read the sentences and choose the best words for the blanks.**

1 Mr. Jackson wants to buy a **plot** of _____ so that he can build a house on it.

a. office   b. land   c. building   d. trees

2 Technology is **transforming** the industry, so it is _____ by improving a lot.

a. occurring   b. reducing   c. appearing   d. changing

3 If you can **secure** the deal, you will _____ a lot of money for the company.

a. spend   b. obtain   c. borrow   d. approve

B **Choose the words from the box to complete the sentences.**

schooling	freighter	ecofriendly	abandoned	withstand

1 The building is able to _____ high winds and earthquakes.

2 The _____ takes about two weeks to sail across the ocean.

3 Many of the homes in the town were _____ over the years.

4 Thanks to his _____, he learned how to become a good designer.

5 The architect is focusing on creating _____ designs of buildings.

Translation

C **Read the sentences and translate them into your language.**

1 Their only real weakness is that they are made of steel so can rust.

→ _____

2 In some urban areas, landowners rent tiny plots of land for people to put their homes on.

→ _____

3 Some architects have made creative designs by arranging multiple containers into unique shapes.

→ _____

Paraphrasing

D **Paraphrase the sentences from the passage with the words and phrases in the box.**

perfect	across water	large sums of money
high-paying positions	transport items	live in they graduate

1 Shipping containers are used to move goods on freighters across the oceans.

→ Freighters _____ in shipping containers _____.

2 After young people complete their schooling, they often cannot secure well-paying jobs.

→ Lots of young people cannot get _____ after _____.

3 The compact sizes of shipping container homes therefore make them ideal places to reside in.

→ Shipping container homes are small, which makes them _____ places to

_____.

4 That is much less than the hundreds of thousands—or even millions—of dollars that homes sell for in some urban areas.

→ That is much less than the _____ houses in cities sell for.

Listening

E **Listen to the summary and fill in the blanks.**

Young people often cannot afford houses in ❶ _____, so some of them are moving in to shipping container homes. Shipping containers are used to ❷ _____ goods on freighters, so they are ❸ _____. People are ❹ _____ them into homes. They are ❺ _____ than houses in urban areas. Young people are often ❻ _____ so do not need much space. Since shipping container homes are small, they are ❼ _____ for young people. People who need more ❽ _____ can put two or more shipping containers together. Making homes from these objects also helps the ❾ _____ by ❿ _____ steel.

Unit 3 **Ancient Burial Methods**

Vocabulary

A **Read the sentences and choose the best words for the blanks.**

1 They will **date** the objects to try to find out how _____ they are.

    a. old   b. expensive   c. rare   d. unique

2 The **deceased** were buried in graves since they were no longer _____.

    a. working   b. alive   c. sick   d. interested

3 The archaeologist found an **intact** vase that had not been _____ at all.

    a. buried   b. sold   c. painted   d. damaged

B **Choose the words from the box to complete the sentences.**

mummy	hominid	underworld	cemetery	rite

1 Neanderthals are a type of ancient _____.

2 They will hold a funeral _____ for the dead man.

3 They found many dead bodies in the old _____.

4 King Tut's _____ was found in excellent condition.

5 The Greeks and Romans believed the dead went to the _____.

Translation

C **Read the sentences and translate them into your language.**

1 Since prehistoric times, humans have buried people when they die.

    ➜ _____

2 Their bodies were well preserved thanks to the dry climate in the Egyptian desert.

    ➜ _____

3 After all, many cultures considered the underworld to be where the souls of the departed went.

    ➜ _____

Paraphrasing

D **Paraphrase the sentences from the passage with the words and phrases in the box.**

important	put the deceased	together with items
inside containers	religions of people	reach the afterlife

1 People in ancient cultures often buried their dead with objects from the deceased's life.

→ The dead were often buried _____ from the lives during ancient times.

2 During the republic years, the Romans burned their dead and placed the ashes in urns.

→ Romans in the republic years burned bodies and put the ashes _____.

3 Some think they may have buried their dead in the ground to send them to the afterlife more easily.

→ Some guess they _____ in graves so that they could easily _____.

4 Eventually, burying people took on a religious meaning in many cultures around the world.

→ Over time, burying the dead became _____ in the _____ around the world.

Listening

E **Listen to the summary and fill in the blanks.**

Humans have been ❶ _____ the dead ever since ❷ _____ times.
They might have buried the dead to make it easier for them to get to the ❸ _____
in the underworld. The oldest buried human ❹ _____ were found in a cave in
Israel. The remains have been ❺ _____ to 100,000 B.C. The ancient Egyptians
buried people in the ground and also made ❻ _____ to preserve people's bodies.
During the Roman Republic, the Romans ❼ _____ their dead and put the
❽ _____ in urns. During the Roman Empire, however, they buried people
❾ _____ to the ❿ _____ of Christianity.

Unit 4 Dragons in Eastern and Western Mythology

Vocabulary

A **Read the sentences and choose the best words for the blanks.**

1 People **worshiped** their gods by _____ them inside temples.

a. praying to   b. looking at   c. traveling to   d. talking about

2 The **gigantic** monster was so _____ that everyone was afraid of it.

a. ugly   b. important   c. huge   d. noisy

3 He **plunged** from the mountain and _____ into the river far below.

a. swam   b. fell   c. stared   d. grew

B **Choose the words from the box to complete the sentences.**

treasure	fearsome	kidnapped	serpent	mythology

1 The _____ tried to kill the man by biting him.

2 The dragon is sleeping on a huge pile of _____.

3 A dragon _____ the princess and took her to its lair.

4 Dragons are common creatures in Western _____.

5 The hero had to fight many _____ monsters during his life.

Translation

C **Read the sentences and translate them into your language.**

1 A dragon is a magical animal capable of various feats.

➡ _____

2 Unlike Eastern dragons, they can breathe fire, so they avoid watery places, which can kill them.

➡ _____

3 *Saint George and the Dragon* is one story about the killing of a dragon that had kidnapped a princess.

➡ _____

Paraphrasing

D **Paraphrase the sentences from the passage with the words and phrases in the box.**

resemble	appear in legends	scared of
different	bring good fortune	pray to dragons

1 A Chinese dragon has body parts similar to those of other animals.

→ The bodies of Chinese dragons _____ those of various animals.

2 In Western cultures, dragons were not worshiped but feared.

→ People in the West did not _____ but were _____ them.

3 In Eastern cultures, dragons are important mythical creatures and are believed to be lucky.

→ In the East, people think dragons are important creatures in myth and _____.

4 It features in the mythologies of Eastern and Western cultures, yet the dragon is not the same in these places.

→ Dragons _____ from the East and the West, but they are _____ in each place.

Listening

E **Listen to the summary and fill in the blanks.**

Dragons are magical ❶ _____ that appear in the ❷ _____ of Eastern and Western cultures. In Eastern cultures such as China, dragons look like ❸ _____. They have the body ❹ _____ of other animals and live in lakes and oceans or high in clouds. Western dragons look like ❺ _____ lizards and can ❻ _____ fire. In Eastern cultures, dragons are ❼ _____ to be lucky, and they can control the weather and make rain fall. In Western cultures, dragons are ❽ _____ because they are ❾ _____ creatures. There are stories about ❿ _____ who try to kill dragons.

Unit 5 **Singing Sand**

Vocabulary

A   **Read the sentences and choose the best words for the blanks.**

1 Climbing a sand **dune** is like going up and down a small _____.

   a. road   b. tunnel   c. bridge   d. hill

2 When we heard the **rumbling** sound, we thought it was _____ in the distance.

   a. rain   b. light   c. music   d. thunder

3 The animal makes an **audible** noise, but it is hard to _____ the sound sometimes.

   a. remember   b. imitate   c. hear   d. understand

B   **Choose the words from the box to complete the sentences.**

accumulated	collide	avalanche	phenomenon	tumbling

1 All of the rocks are _____ to the ground.

2 A spark is produced when two stones _____.

3 Sand has _____ on the beach for thousands of years.

4 This is an interesting _____ and must be studied more.

5 The loud sound caused a(n) _____ to start on the mountain.

Translation

C   **Read the sentences and translate them into your language.**

1 They heard loud, low, rumbling noises coming from sand dunes in these places.

   → _____

2 Some sand dunes create sound multiple times a day while others make noise less frequently.

   → _____

3 Scientists speculate that as sand moves down a dune, individual grains collide with one another.

   → _____

Paraphrasing

D **Paraphrase the sentences from the passage with the words and phrases in the box.**

happens	adventurer	no moisture	causing it
around the world	almost the same	not be blowing	

1 The wind must be still, and the sand must be hot and dry.

→ The wind should _____, and there must be hot sand with _____.

2 There are only around thirty-five places worldwide known to produce singing sand.

→ _____, singing sand only _____ in about thirty-five places.

3 A close analysis revealed that the Moroccan grains of sand were nearly identical in size.

→ Research showed that the Moroccan sands were _____ size.

4 Marco Polo, the great thirteenth-century Italian explorer, believed evil spirits were responsible.

→ Marco Polo, an Italian _____ from the 1200s, thought evil spirits were

_____.

Listening

E **Listen to the summary and fill in the blanks.**

People have been hearing low, ❶ _____ sounds in some deserts for thousands of years. This singing sand only happens in around thirty-five places around the world. Scientists have done some ❷ _____ on it ❸ _____. They learned that singing sand happens when the wind is ❹ _____, and the sand is hot and dry. When sand ❺ _____ down the ❻ _____, it creates sound. But the ❼ _____ can be different. Scientists ❽ _____ that the sizes of the ❾ _____ of sand cause different sounds. When falling sand ❿ _____ with other grains of sand, it makes singing sand.

Unit 6 **Volcanic Eruptions**

Vocabulary

A **Read the sentences and choose the best words for the blanks.**

1 A large cloud of ash **consumed** the land and _____ everything it touched.

a. destroyed   b. attacked   c. removed   d. froze

2 Because lava is **fluid**, it can _____ swiftly down the sides of a volcano.

a. melt   b. flow   c. erupt   d. harden

3 After the **lava** came out of the volcano, the hot _____ destroyed everything in their way.

a. gases   b. ashes   c. rocks   d. air

B **Choose the words from the box to complete the sentences.**

inhabited	destructive	eruption	observe	spewing

1 Volcanoes are some of nature's most _____ forces.

2 The volcano has been _____ lava for several hours.

3 The small island is _____ by around a hundred people.

4 Many people visit Hawaii to _____ the active volcanoes there.

5 The _____ of Mount Saint Helens in 1980 killed more than fifty people.

Translation

C **Read the sentences and translate them into your language.**

1 Geologists have identified several types of eruptions.

→ _____

2 Still, Strombolian eruptions can be dangerous if they take place near inhabited areas.

→ _____

3 The reason a volcano erupts in this manner is that the magma inside it has large bubbles of gas.

→ _____

Paraphrasing

D **Paraphrase the sentences from the passage with the words and phrases in the box.**

constantly	violent and visible	shoot lava
can expel lava	destroy the city	in the air

1 Called lava fountains, streams of lava can rise more than 300 meters high.

➡ Lava fountains can _____ over 300 meters _____.

2 In 79 A.D., he saw the eruption of Mount Vesuvius, which consumed the nearby city Pompeii.

➡ He saw Mount Vesuvius erupt and _____ Pompeii in 79 A.D.

3 Hawaiian, Strombolian, and Plinian eruptions are among the most explosive and noticeable.

➡ The most _____ eruptions are Hawaiian, Strombolian, and Plinian ones.

4 Some volcanoes shoot large amounts of lava hundreds of meters high, yet they do not erupt continually.

➡ Some volcanoes _____ hundreds of meters high, but they do not erupt

_____.

Listening

E **Listen to the summary and fill in the blanks.**

Volcanic ❶ _____ spew gas, ash, rocks, and ❷ _____ into the air.
There are several types of eruptions. The Hawaiian eruption can ❸ _____ shoot
lava ❹ _____ into the air for years. This lava is ❺ _____, so it
❻ _____ great distances. Strombolian eruptions ❼ _____ lava into
the air, but they erupt every few minutes. They are ❽ _____ eruptions but are not
violent. Plinian eruptions were ❾ _____ by Pliny the Younger when he saw Mount
Vesuvius erupt. These shoot gas and ash high into the air. They create ❿ _____
flows that destroy everything in their way, too.

Unit 7 Cottage Industries

Vocabulary

A **Read the sentences and choose the best words for the blanks.**

1 They **are engaged in** the community, so they will _____ the upcoming festival.

a. take part in   b. visit   c. ignore   d. vary

2 Everyone loved the _____ that the **caterer** provided for the party.

a. decorations   b. music   c. food   d. entertainment

3 Judy can **sew** well since she learned to use _____ as a child.

a. a computer   b. a needle and thread   c. a fork and a knife   d. a pen and a pencil

B **Choose the words from the box to complete the sentences.**

mass-produce	necessities	textiles	inefficient	specializes in

1 Some goods are _____ that people must have.

2 It is _____ to make complicated machines by oneself.

3 Henry Ford used the assembly line to _____ automobiles.

4 The economist _____ the study of international markets.

5 During the Industrial Revolution, people used machines to make _____ and clothing.

Translation

C **Read the sentences and translate them into your language.**

1 Today, the majority of goods around the world are mass-produced in factories.

→ _____

2 Since items were made in people's homes, that is how the name cottage industry was created.

→ _____

3 Thanks to the Internet, which lets people sell to buyers around the world, it is once again possible for cottage industries to thrive.

→ _____

Paraphrasing

D **Paraphrase the sentences from the passage with the words and phrases in the box.**

| began | food preparation | were not large |
| inexpensive | examples | moved to | took a long time |

1 Since one person made the entire item, manufacturing was a very slow process.

→ Because each item was made by one person, making goods _____.

2 People did not have to spend large amounts of money starting business since they were so small.

→ Starting businesses was _____ because they _____.

3 In the 1700s, the Industrial Revolution started in England and then spread to other countries.

→ The Industrial Revolution _____ in England in the 1700s and _____ other nations later.

4 Food providers such as bakers and caterers operate as cottage industries.

→ Bakers and caterers in the _____ industry are _____ of cottage industries.

Listening

E **Listen to the summary and fill in the blanks.**

Once the Industrial Revolution began in the 1700s, people began to ❶ _____ items. Before then, most ❷ _____ was done in cottage industries. These were small homes where people both lived and ❸ _____. People made cloth, ❹ _____, nails, and other necessities in them. The ❺ _____ of goods made in cottage industries ❻ _____, and manufacturing was a slow process. But people could work out of their homes, spend ❼ _____ money starting businesses, and get jobs. Most cottage industries could not ❽ _____ against factories, so they ❾ _____. But the Internet can let some cottage industries ❿ _____ today.

Unit 8 **The Economic Cycle**

Vocabulary

A **Read the sentences and choose the best words for the blanks.**

1 The material began to **shrink**, so it became much _____ than before.
   a. heavier   b. prettier   c. more expensive   d. smaller

2 He requested a **loan** from his friend because he needed some _____.
   a. time   b. money   c. fun   d. jobs

3 The county is suffering from **inflation**, so prices are _____ these days.
   a. falling   b. rising   c. staying the same   d. changing

B **Choose the words from the box to complete the sentences.**

unemployment	salary	booming	investment	bankruptcy

1 A(n) _____ in gold or silver is often a smart choice.

2 He makes a good _____ at his job as an airplane pilot.

3 The country's economy is getting better, so it is _____ now.

4 The company declared _____ and then went out of business.

5 Because companies do not hire more workers, _____ is increasing.

Translation

C **Read the sentences and translate them into your language.**

1 Economists have identified several stages economies go through.

   → _____

2 Interest rates rise, too, making fewer people apply for loans.

   → _____

3 The four stages of the economic cycle last for various amounts of time.

   → _____

Paraphrasing

D Paraphrase the sentences from the passage with the words and phrases in the box.

a time	good about	take out loans	shrinks
put money into	increasing in size	gets better	

1 Individuals feel confident in the economy, which helps it improve.

→ People feel _____ the economy, so it _____.

2 While the economy is still getting larger, it is not doing so at a rapid pace.

→ Although the economy is getting bigger, it is not _____ quickly.

3 This is a period when an economy gets smaller for at least six months.

→ This is _____ when an economy _____ for six or more months.

4 Interest rates are low, so people borrow more and invest in the stock market.

→ Low interest rates help people _____ and _____ the stock market.

Listening

E Listen to the summary and fill in the blanks.

There are four ❶ _____ in the economic cycle: expansion, slowdown,

❷ _____, and recovery. An economy ❸ _____ during the expansion

stage. People are ❹ _____ in the economy, have jobs, and are making more money.

When a ❺ _____ occurs, an economy improves more slowly while consumer

❻ _____ falls. This leads to a recession, which is a time when the economy gets

smaller for six months or more. People ❼ _____ their jobs and are less

confident in the economy. When a recession ends, a recovery begins. More people get

❽ _____ as companies make ❾ _____. People can spend more money

and ❿ _____ as well.

Unit 9 Modern Surveillance Societies

Vocabulary

A Read the sentences and choose the best words for the blanks.

1 The spy was under **surveillance**, so somebody was constantly _____ him.

    a. watching   b. talking to   c. chasing   d. attacking

2 He is **amassing** supplies and _____ as many of them as he can.

    a. selling   b. building   c. studying   d. collecting

3 The planets **orbit** the sun by moving around it in a shape like a _____.

    a. circle   b. square   c. triangle   d. diamond

B Choose the words from the box to complete the sentences.

violating	privacy	satellite	monitor	repeal

1 The citizens want the government to _____ the law.

2 The _____ is able to spy on people from high above the ground.

3 These days, video cameras often _____ the actions of people.

4 All people should have a right to _____ in their own homes.

5 Some government officials are _____ people's rights nowadays.

Translation

C Read the sentences and translate them into your language.

1 It is difficult to walk anywhere in the city without being caught on camera.

→ _____

2 So many groups and individuals have been fighting back against surveillance states.

→ _____

3 At present, England and China have the world's most comprehensive mass-surveillance societies.

→ _____

Paraphrasing

D **Paraphrase the sentences from the passage with the words and phrases in the box.**

visit	watched closely	get disconnected
nowadays	legalize these activities	allow the collection

1 They have laws which make gathering all of the information legal.

→ They have laws that _____ of all kinds of data.

2 They are upset since they never voted to make these activities be legal.

→ They are angry because they did not vote to _____.

3 These days, the mass surveillance of people is common in some countries.

→ _____, in some nations, people are _____.

4 When users log on to certain websites, they are cut off from the Internet.

→ Users _____ from the Internet if they _____ some webpages.

Listening

E **Listen to the summary and fill in the blanks.**

The mass surveillance of people has increased all around the world. There are cameras

❶ _____ people in cities and ❷ _____ that take pictures from high

above the Earth. People's cellphones are also ❸ _____ . England and China have

the most ❹ _____ mass-surveillance societies. There are security cameras

❺ _____ in London. The Chinese government uses cameras and controls Internet

❻ _____ , too. Other countries have ❼ _____ making it

❽ _____ to watch over citizens. Some people are fighting back ❾ _____

surveillance states. They are trying to get many laws ❿ _____ .

Unit 10 **Deep-Sea Vehicles**

Vocabulary

A **Read the sentences and choose the best words for the blanks.**

1 The vehicle is **autonomous**, so it is capable of running _____.

a. all day long   b. on batteries   c. on gasoline   d. by itself

2 They will **illuminate** the area by using several _____ to let people see.

a. computers   b. robots   c. lights   d. vehicles

3 The **sediment** at the bottom of the ocean resulted in _____ getting into the machine.

a. pollution   b. stones   c. fish   d. sand

B **Choose the words from the box to complete the sentences.**

detach	arguably	manned	free-fall	sonar

1 It is _____ the biggest submarine in the world.

2 The ship is using _____ to detect objects under the water.

3 The vehicle will _____ all the way to the bottom of the ocean.

4 He must _____ the weights for the vehicle to rise to the surface.

5 The _____ vehicle descended to the ocean bottom and took many pictures.

Translation

C **Read the sentences and translate them into your language.**

1 When the pilot wants to resurface, he detaches the weights.

➜ _____

2 They have stayed underwater for as long as seven days and have explored places around the world.

➜ _____

3 Due to the great depths and intense pressure far beneath the surface, exploring the deep sea is difficult.

➜ _____

Paraphrasing

D   **Paraphrase the sentences from the passage with the words and phrases in the box.**

	running alone	two-thirds	above the water
attached to	some say	the entire planet	best-known

1 These machines are programmed to operate all by themselves without any humans.

→ These machines are capable of _____ without humans.

2 The Earth's five oceans cover more than seventy percent of the surface of the planet.

→ The five oceans on the Earth cover more than _____ of _____.

3 Arguably the most famous is the manned deep-sea vehicle *Deepsea Challenger*.

→ _____ the *Deepsea Challenger* is the _____ manned deep-sea vehicle.

4 A pilot on the surface controls them through a cable 10 kilometers long that connects the vessels.

→ A pilot _____ controls them with a very long cable _____ the vessels.

Listening

E   **Listen to the summary and fill in the blanks.**

The oceans cover most of the ❶ _____ surface and average 3,600 meters in ❷ _____. So exploring them is difficult. Some deep-sea vehicles are letting people visit the ❸ _____ of the ocean though. *Deepsea Challenger* is a ❹ _____ vehicle that has ❺ _____ the bottom of Challenger Deep. It can free-fall to the bottom and collect rock, sediment, and ❻ _____ samples. *Medea* and *Jason* are ❼ _____ operated vehicles. They work together and can stay ❽ _____ for as long as seven days. AUVs are ❾ _____ underwater vehicles. Scientists are using them to ❿ _____ the mysteries of the deep sea.

Unit 11 **Bird Feathers**

Vocabulary

A **Read the sentences and choose the best words for the blanks.**

1 An eagle can **strike** fish in the water and hit them _____.

a. softly   b. slowly   c. strongly   d. repeatedly

2 A bee **sting** from a _____ part of the bee's body can hurt people.

a. strong   b. hard   c. unique   d. sharp

3 Some birds have **neat** nests that they _____ each day.

a. clean   b. repair   c. bring food to   d. lay eggs in

B **Choose the words from the box to complete the sentences.**

fluffy	function	bends	vital	specialized

1 A bird's wing will break if it _____ too much.

2 It is _____ that birds stay warm during the winter months.

3 Birds have several types of feathers that vary in shape and _____.

4 The bird's _____ feathers help keep it warm and dry in the rain.

5 Feathers have become _____, so there are several types of them.

Translation

C **Read the sentences and translate them into your language.**

1 Feathers are similar to hair since they grow from the skin.

➡ _____

2 Among the most important of bird feathers are called contour feathers.

➡ _____

3 Not all birds have bristles, but they are located around the eyes and mouths of the birds that have them.

➡ _____

Paraphrasing

D Paraphrase the sentences from the passage with the phrases in the box.

various purposes	bend in flight	the most vital	
have gathered	different in	hundreds of years	can fly

1 There are other types of feathers, but those are four of the most important ones.

→ Birds have other kinds of feathers, but those four are _____.

2 These feathers come in a wide variety of shapes, sizes, and colors, and they also have different purposes.

→ The feathers are _____ shape, size, and color and have _____, too.

3 They must be light and strong to enable birds to achieve flight, so they frequently bend as birds fly but rarely break.

→ They have to be light and strong so that birds _____, so they often _____ but do not usually break.

4 These feathers have been collected by people for centuries to use in pillows and mattresses thanks to their softness.

→ People _____ these feathers for _____ to make soft pillows and mattresses.

Listening

E Listen to the summary and fill in the blanks.

Over millions of years, different types of feathers have ❶ _____ on birds.
❷ _____ feathers are large and include ❸ _____ feathers and tail
feathers. They can ❹ _____ since they let birds fly. They protect birds from the
sun, wind, rain, and ❺ _____ objects. ❻ _____ feathers are soft and
❼ _____ and keep birds warm and dry. Water birds such as ducks, geese, and
swans have them. Semiplumes are ❽ _____ between contour feathers. They
❾ _____ birds and give them their shape. Some birds have stiff bristles around their
eyes and mouths. Bristles protect these birds from harmful ❿ _____.

Unit 12 **Walking Fish**

Vocabulary

A **Read the sentences and choose the best words for the blanks.**

1 The **lungs** are important to animals since they let them _____.
   a. smell   b. breathe   c. touch   d. taste

2 The fish **utilizes** its fins to move and _____ its nostrils to breathe.
   a. causes   b. carries   c. uses   d. produces

3 Before diving under the water, he **gulped** several times to take in some _____.
   a. air   b. food   c. water   d. smells

B **Choose the words from the box to complete the sentences.**

extensive	gills	possess	transition	depart

1 Most sharks _____ a large fin on their backs.

2 The fish will _____ their breeding grounds next month.

3 Thanks to _____, fish are able to breathe in the water.

4 Fish cannot spend a(n) _____ amount of time out of water.

5 The animal must make a(n) _____ from being a baby to being an adult.

Translation

C **Read the sentences and translate them into your language.**

1 Many biologists believe life on the Earth originated in the oceans.

   → _____

2 Likewise, it migrates in times when droughts dry up the pond or lake it lives in.

   → _____

3 Some species of lungfish have nostrils while others breathe through their mouths by gulping air.

   → _____

Paraphrasing

D   Paraphrase the sentences from the passage with the words and phrases in the box.

need	has lungs	not enough oxygen	on land
leaving	extract oxygen	place to live	animals evolved

1   Land animals require lungs to breathe air whereas fish utilize gills to remove oxygen from the water.

→ Land animals _____ lungs to breathe air, but fish have gills to _____ from the water.

2   The snakehead possesses lungs and can often be found migrating out of water in certain situations.

→ The snakehead _____ and sometimes migrates _____ at various times.

3   Biologists hope to understand how animals changed when they departed the water many years ago.

→ Biologists think they can understand how _____ after _____ the water in the past.

4   When the water it lives in lacks enough oxygen, it will travel across small areas of land in search of better conditions.

→ If there is _____ in the water it lives in, it will move across land to find a better _____.

Listening

E   Listen to the summary and fill in the blanks.

Scientists believe walking fish are ❶ _____ that animals evolved from being ocean ❷ _____ to land creatures. The lungfish has both ❸ _____ and gills, so it can ❹ _____ in water and on land. It can use its ❺ _____ like arms and legs to move on land. The snakehead also has lungs. It can ❻ _____ on land to find better living ❼ _____. It ❽ _____ on the ground like a snake. The mudskipper spends around ❾ _____ percent of its life on land. It can climb trees and jump. Biologists say that it acts more like a ❿ _____ animal than a fish.

Unit 13 **Yellow Journalism and Muckraking**

Vocabulary

A **Read the sentences and choose the best words for the blanks.**

1 Newspapers use **sensational** headlines to get _____ from their readers.

  a. advertisements   b. reactions   c. subscriptions   d. complaints

2 The police **blamed** the man for the crash and said he was _____ everything.

  a. responsible for   b. upset about   c. involved in   d. happy with

3 The **scandal** harmed the reporter's _____, so nobody believed anything he wrote.

  a. work   b. corruption   c. life   d. reputation

B **Choose the words from the box to complete the sentences.**

headline	corruption	go undercover	profession	reform

1 People in the journalism _____ need to be good writers.

2 The newspaper tried to reveal _____ in the police force.

3 The _____ of the paper reads that the country is going to war.

4 She is trying to _____ the government, but it is difficult to do so.

5 He will _____ in order to investigate the problems in the government.

Translation

C **Read the sentences and translate them into your language.**

1 The written word was particularly important then since there was no radio or TV.

  → _____

2 They were trying to find the truth to reform society through their muckraking.

  → _____

3 The stories were often about crimes and scandals, yet there was usually little truth to them.

  → _____

Paraphrasing

D **Paraphrase the sentences from the passage with the words and phrases in the box.**

> convinced   lots of competition   centuries
> underwent   positive changes   go to war   learn about

1 At the end of the nineteenth century, the newspaper industry was very competitive.

→ By the end of the 1800s, there was _____ between newspapers.

2 Thanks to them, there were many positive reforms made in American society.

→ Due to their actions, American society _____ some _____.

3 During the 1700s and 1800s, most people got their news by reading newspapers and magazines.

→ In the eighteenth and nineteenth _____, people read newspapers and magazines
to _____ the news.

4 Their headlines and stories helped encourage the American people to get the U.S. government to declare war on Spain.

→ The headlines and stories _____ Americans to make the U.S. government
_____ against Spain.

Listening

E **Listen to the summary and fill in the blanks.**

> In the United States in the 1700s and 1800s, many people got their ❶ _____
> from newspapers. In the late 1800s, yellow journalism started. It ❷ _____
> sensational headlines and stories that had little ❸ _____. The newspapers of Joseph
> Pulitzer and William Randolph Hearst ❹ _____ yellow journalism. They even got the
> American people to desire war ❺ _____ Spain. Other journalists were muckrakers.
> They wrote about ❻ _____ and ❼ _____ in society. They wanted to
> ❽ _____ society. Their stories were often ❾ _____ in magazines.
> Some muckrakers went ❿ _____ to learn about problems in certain industries.

Unit 14 **Citizen Journalism**

Vocabulary

A **Read the sentences and choose the best words for the blanks.**

1 The teacher **criticized** the student's work and made some _____ comments about it.

a. bad   b. nice   c. helpful   d. positive

2 People **distrust** reporters nowadays because they cannot _____ what they say or write.

a. understand   b. remember   c. approve of   d. believe

3 The _____ in the **audience** all stood up and clapped when the performance ended.

a. amateurs   b. actors   c. people   d. reporters

B **Choose the words from the box to complete the sentences.**

mass media	publication	hits	disaster	biased

1 Many people do not trust the _____ these days.

2 Citizen journalists like to get many _____ on their websites.

3 It was a _____ when the bridge collapsed and fell into the river.

4 The *Wall Street Journal* is a popular _____ in the United States.

5 Too many reporters are _____ and write articles based on their politics.

Translation

C **Read the sentences and translate them into your language.**

1 Citizen journalists are often the first to report on breaking news.

➜ _____

2 Most blogs have small audiences, yet others get thousands of hits a day.

➜ _____

3 But these days, citizen journalists are able to publish their stories on the Internet.

➜ _____

Paraphrasing

D **Paraphrase the sentences from the passage with the words and phrases in the box.**

| prejudiced | links it | participate in | was consumed |
| because of | can be read | believe reporters | |

1 They distrust mass media due to the biased reporting of many journalists.

→ They do not _____ because so many of them are _____ .

2 Thanks to modern technology, regular people now engage in what is called citizen journalism.

→ _____ modern technology, anyone can _____ citizen journalism.

3 Before the creation of the World Wide Web, the only way to spread mass media was through print.

→ Before the Internet, print was the only way mass media _____ .

4 If a news report on a blog is linked by a popular website, it can get millions of hits.

→ A news story on a blog _____ millions of times if a popular webpage

_____ .

Listening

E **Listen to the summary and fill in the blanks.**

Most journalism was ❶ _____ by ❷ _____ in the 1900s, but this is changing. Thanks to the World Wide Web, there are now citizen journalists. Many of them use blogs to ❸ _____ stories, and others ❹ _____ videos onto the Internet. Some citizen journalists work ❺ _____ , but others only work for a day. They may use Facebook or Twitter to report on ❻ _____ news stories. Young people often ❼ _____ mass media but trust citizen journalists. However, professional journalists ❽ _____ citizen journalists and say their reporting is ❾ _____ in ❿ _____ .

Unit 15 Water in the Solar System

Vocabulary

A **Read the sentences and choose the best words for the blanks.**

1 During the **mission**, the _____ will take several people to the space station.

   a. satellite   b. spacecraft   c. planet   d. missile

2 The _____ that appears when water boils is a form of **water vapor**.

   a. steam   b. bubble   c. liquid   d. ice

3 There are billions of **asteroids** in the solar system, and they are made of various _____.

   a. minerals   b. gems   c. metals   d. rocks

B **Choose the words from the box to complete the sentences.**

satellite	telescope	estimate	solar system	abundance

1 Jupiter is the largest planet in the _____.

2 Galileo used a(n) _____ to look at the moon.

3 Water exists in _____ on some moons and planets.

4 Venus does not have a(n) _____, and neither does Mercury.

5 Astronomers _____ that there are billions of stars in the galaxy.

Translation

C **Read the sentences and translate them into your language.**

1 Of the eight major planets, water exists on the surface of both Earth and Mars.

  ➡ _____

2 Astronomers also think that water is present in the interiors of the gas giants.

  ➡ _____

3 Ganymede, another of Jupiter's moons, has an even larger ocean of liquid water under its surface.

  ➡ _____

Paraphrasing

D **Paraphrase the sentences from the passage with the phrases in the box.**

the data	its frozen form	the majority of	see very far
not only	plenty of	at its two poles	also exists

1 Water can be found on many asteroids, primarily in the form of ice, too.

→ _____ asteroids have water in _____ .

2 Most of the information collected so far has come from long-range telescopes.

→ Telescopes that can _____ have gathered most of _____ .

3 Most of Mars's frozen water is located at its northern and southern poles in the form of large ice caps.

→ _____ the ice on Mars is at the big ice caps _____ .

4 In addition to being on the Earth in abundance, there is water on planets, moons, and asteroids in the solar system.

→ There is _____ lots of water on the Earth, but it _____ on planets, moons, and asteroids in the solar system.

Listening

E **Listen to the summary and fill in the blanks.**

In the ❶ _____ , water in all three ❷ _____ is on the Earth and in other places. Water is on the ❸ _____ of Earth and Mars. Most of the water on Mars's surface is ice at its northern and southern ❹ _____ . Some moons have water. Europa and Ganymede, two of ❺ _____ moons, may have enormous liquid ❻ _____ beneath their surfaces. There is ice on many ❼ _____ , and there are also ice crystals in the ❽ _____ of Jupiter, Saturn, Uranus, and Neptune. NASA and the European Space Agency will send ❾ _____ to Europa to look for water ❿ _____ .

Unit 16 **Galaxies and Their Formation**

Vocabulary

A **Read the sentences and choose the best words for the blanks.**

1 An **irregular** object does not have a fixed or _____ shape.

a. far   b. even   c. round   d. large

2 You must sweep the **dust** to get all of the _____ off the floor.

a. objects   b. toys   c. material   d. dirt

3 Some astronomers think the universe is **expanding**, so it is getting _____ all the time.

a. bigger   b. hotter   c. denser   d. smaller

B **Choose the words from the box to complete the sentences.**

universe	comprise	massive	elliptical	rotate

1 Uranus is 14.5 times more _____ than Earth.

2 Nobody knows exactly how big the _____ is.

3 It takes Earth about twenty-four hours to _____ once.

4 The orbits of the planets are not circular but are _____ in shape.

5 The sun and the eight planets and their moon _____ the solar system.

Translation

C **Read the sentences and translate them into your language.**

1 Spiral galaxies have several long arms that spiral around the center.

→ _____

2 Galaxies started being created after the formation of the universe.

→ _____

3 In the past, people believed that all the stars in the universe were located in a single group.

→ _____

Paraphrasing

D Paraphrase the sentences from the passage with the words and phrases in the box.

getting bigger	countless number	moving in circles
hit	might be formed	going around	one small point

1 When the clouds collapsed due to gravity, they formed rotating disks.

→ Gravity made the clouds collapse and form disks _____ .

2 They are thought to be created when two galaxies collide with each other.

→ They _____ when two galaxies _____ each other.

3 A galaxy is an enormous group of stars and the objects that orbit them.

→ A galaxy has a _____ of stars and objects _____ them.

4 All the matter in the universe was contained in a tiny point that suddenly started to expand rapidly.

→ _____ contained all the matter in the universe, and then it began _____ quickly.

Listening

E Listen to the summary and fill in the blanks.

> Galaxies are ❶ _____ groups of stars. Many contain ❷ _____ of stars, and most of them have a massive black hole in their center. There are four ❸ _____ types of galaxies. ❹ _____ galaxies and barred spiral galaxies both have arms. Elliptical galaxies have somewhat ❺ _____ shapes while ❻ _____ galaxies have many different shapes. Galaxies did not form until after the Big Bang created the ❼ _____ . There were clouds of hydrogen, helium, and dust that ❽ _____ and made stars. Then, ❾ _____ disks formed, and that made more stars form. When enough stars were created, galaxies ❿ _____ .

Further
Writing Practice

Unit 1 **Sustainable Architecture**

Q **Do you know a building that uses sustainable architecture? What features make the building sustainable?**

A The following table shows some ideas for answering the question above. Check the one that you like the most. If you have your own idea, write it in the last row.

Building	Features
☐ Shanghai Tower	• The skyscraper in Shanghai, China, has a unique shape that lets it reduce wind resistance. • It also uses renewable energy and has landscaping that makes it cooler. These and other features reduce the amount of energy it uses by 21%.
☐ Bahrain World Trade Center	• This building in Bahrain has fifty floors and two towers. • It has three sky bridges connecting the towers, and each has a wind turbine attached to it. Combined, they create around 15% of the electricity used in the building.
☐ Bank of America Tower	• This building in New York City in the USA uses recycled construction materials. • It also harvests rainwater by catching it and has windows going from the floor to ceiling to insulate the building better.

B Use one of the ideas in A and write a short paragraph by using the idea.

One building that uses sustainable architecture is _____. The building _____
_____ .

It _____
_____ .

Unit 2 Shipping Container Homes

Q   **What is a unique type of home some people live in? What features make it unique?**

A   The following table shows some ideas for answering the question above. Check the one that you like the most. If you have your own idea, write it in the last row.

Home	Features
☐ cave house	• In Cappadocia in Turkey, there are rock formations that have produced numerous caves. • People build houses in the caves. The thick walls keep people warm during cold winters and cool during hot summers.
☐ igloo	• In Canada and Greenland, the large amounts of snow and ice are used as building materials for some people. • People use blocks of snow to create igloos. A short tunnel at the entrance reduces the effects of the wind and prevents heat from being lost.
☐ yurt	• In Mongolia, there are homes that people can pick up and take with them wherever they go. • People build houses like a large tent with a wooden frame and thick fabric covering it. It is usually big and round and can be quite comfortable to live in.

B   Use one of the ideas in A and write a short paragraph by using the idea.

Some people live in _____ . In _____

_____ .

People _____

_____

_____ .

Unit 3 Ancient Burial Methods

Q **What is done with some people's bodies after they die in modern times?**

A The following table shows some ideas for answering the question above. Check the one that you like the most. If you have your own idea, write it in the last row.

Action	Description
☐ cryonics	• A person's body is frozen after death. • This is done because the person believes that medicine in the future may improve enough to attempt to bring dead people back to life.
☐ space burial	• The body of a dead person is burned, and then part of the person's remains is shot into space. • This is done because the person has a connection to outer space such as studying it or wanting to visit it someday.
☐ plastination	• A body is preserved by replacing the water and fat in it with plastic. • This is done because the person wants to donate his or her body to medical science to be displayed for educational purposes.

B Use one of the ideas in A and write a short paragraph by using the idea.

In modern times, some people use _____ . In this case, a/the body _____

_____ .

This is done because _____

_____

_____ .

Unit 4 Dragons in Eastern and Western Mythology

Q **What is a dragon that you know about? Where does the dragon appear, and what are its characteristics?**

A The following table shows some ideas for answering the question above. Check the one that you like the most. If you have your own idea, write it in the last row.

Dragon	Characteristics
☐ Dragon	• Dragon appears in the *Shrek* movies. • Dragon is ruby colored and protects a castle with Princess Fiona in it. She becomes married to Donkey and appears in several *Shrek* movies.
☐ Toothless	• Toothless appears in the movie *How to Train Your Dragon*. • Toothless is injured by the Viking teenager Hiccup. Toothless teaches Hiccup about dragons, and together with others, they help defeat the terrible dragon Red Death.
☐ Nidhogg	• Nidhogg appears in Norse mythology. • Nidhogg chews at one of the three roots of Yggdrasil, the world tree. The tree is important for connecting the nine worlds in Norse mythology.

B Use one of the ideas in A and write a short paragraph by using the idea.

One dragon I know about is _____. This dragon _____

_____.

It _____

_____

_____.

Unit 5 Singing Sand

Q What is an interesting feature found in some deserts? What are its characteristics?

A The following table shows some ideas for answering the question above. Check the one that you like the most. If you have your own idea, write it in the last row.

Feature	Characteristics
☐ oasis	• This is a place in a desert where fresh water from underground comes to the surface. • When an oasis appears, a small pond or pool may form. This allows trees and other plants to grow, and many animals visit it to drink water.
☐ sand dune	• This is a small hill that is made of sand. • When the wind blows, it may create a sand dune. Sand dunes are constantly changing shapes, and they may appear or disappear according to how the wind blows.
☐ arroyo	• This is a dry stream or creek bed that may go through a desert. • When it rains, an arroyo may quickly fill with fast-moving water and start a flood.

B Use one of the ideas in A and write a short paragraph by using the idea.

An interesting feature found in some deserts is _____. It is _____
_____ .
One of its characteristics is that _____
_____
_____ .

Unit 6 Volcanic Eruptions

Q What is a volcano that erupted in the past? What were the results of that eruption?

A The following table shows some ideas for answering the question above. Check the one that you like the most. If you have your own idea, write it in the last row.

Volcano	Results
☐ Krakatoa	• It is a volcano in Indonesia that erupted in August 1883. • The eruption was so powerful that it destroyed most of the volcano and could be heard thousands of kilometers away. It caused tsunamis that killed more than 36,000 people.
☐ Toba	• It is a supervolcano in Indonesia that erupted around 75,000 years ago. • The eruption caused the global climate to change and almost made humans go extinct. As a result of the Toba eruption, only around 3,000 to 10,000 humans remained for a while.
☐ El Chichon	• It is a volcano in Mexico that erupted in 1982. • The eruption created pyroclastic flows that destroyed nine villages around the volcano. It killed around 2,000 people and destroyed a large amount of the land around it.

B Use one of the ideas in A and write a short paragraph by using the idea.

One volcano that erupted in the past was _____. It _____
_____.

The eruption _____
_____
_____.

Unit 7 Cottage Industries

Do you know of a product that people make in cottage industries nowadays? How do people make it?

A The following table shows some ideas for answering the question above. Check the one that you like the most. If you have your own idea, write it in the last row.

Product	How It Is Made
☐ candle	• Some people create handmade candles at home businesses. • People make molds for their candles. Then, they pour wax into the molds and let the wax cool. They often sell their items online.
☐ furniture	• Carpenters can make all kinds of wood furniture, including chairs, tables, and beds. • Carpenters create designs for the furniture they want to make. They select the wood, cut it, and then put the pieces together. They often sell their items to local customers.
☐ baked good	• Bakers create many different baked goods, including cakes, cupcakes, bread, and cookies. • Bakers purchase ingredients, follow recipes, and bake various items. They often sell their items at bake sales.

B Use one of the ideas in A and write a short paragraph by using the idea.

One product people make is _____. It is made by _____

_____.

They _____

_____

_____.

Unit 8 The Economic Cycle

Q Do you know of a time when an economy was in a period where it expanded very much? What happened then?

A The following table shows some ideas for answering the question above. Check the one that you like the most. If you have your own idea, write it in the last row.

Economic Period	What Happened
☐ the Roaring Twenties	• This happened in the United States during the 1920s. • World War I had ended, so the economy began expanding. The prices of goods were low, so many people were able to buy them. That made the economy improve for many years.
☐ the Spanish Miracle	• This happened in Spain from around 1959 to 1974. • Spain began to industrialize in many parts. Thanks to a variety of industries, including automobile manufacturing and textiles, the economy of Spain became the world's ninth biggest economy.
☐ the Age of Mercantilism	• This happened in England in the 1700s. • The English engaged in trade from its colonies, especially those in North America. All of the trade went through England, which improved the economy greatly.

B Use one of the ideas in A and write a short paragraph by using the idea.

A period when the economy expanded very much was _____.

It happened _____.

The reason it happened is that _____

_____

_____

Unit 9 **Modern Surveillance Societies**

Q **What is a method that governments can use to engage in mass surveillance? How does it work?**

A The following table shows some ideas for answering the question above. Check the one that you like the most. If you have your own idea, write it in the last row.

Method	How It Works
☐ spy satellite	• A rocket lifts a spy satellite into space, so it begins to orbit the Earth. • The satellite uses cameras that use advanced technology. The cameras can observe very small objects clearly even from hundreds or thousands of kilometers away.
☐ CCTV	• Governments install a closed-circuit television (CCTV) into a place where they can observe people. • They monitor the camera to look for activity that is illegal or possibly dangerous to others.
☐ biometric surveillance	• A person's fingerprints, DNA, or facial characteristics are recorded. • Governments can analyze the data taken from the person and match it to a place where a crime took place. That can help determine if the person committed a crime.

B Use one of the ideas in A and write a short paragraph by using the idea.

One way governments engage in mass surveillance is with _____.

First, _____.

After that, _____

_____

_____.

Unit 10 Deep-Sea Vehicles

Q **What is a vehicle that can go to places that are hard to get to? What features of the vehicle allow it to travel to hard-to-get places?**

A The following table shows some ideas for answering the question above. Check the one that you like the most. If you have your own idea, write it in the last row.

Vehicle	Features
☐ the Caterpillar DN6	• This machine was specially designed to travel to the South Pole in Antarctica. • It survived temperatures as low as -51 degrees Celsius. It kept its crew warm, and it hauled a large amount of supplies.
☐ *Turanor*	• This is the largest solar-powered boat in the world. • Its solar panels provide energy for two electric motors that let it travel up to 19km/hr. In 2012, *Turanor* became the first vehicle that used solar power to travel around the world.
☐ *Unity*	• This is a spacecraft owned by Virgin Galactic. • It sent two men into outer space in 2018. In the future, *Unity* will carry tourists into outer space. It will let them experience zero gravity and allow them to see the Earth from outer space.

B Use one of the ideas in A and write a short paragraph by using the idea.

I know about _____ . It _____

_____ .

It/Its _____

_____

_____ .

Unit 11 **Bird Feathers**

Q What is a bird that has interesting or unique feathers? What makes the feathers so interesting or unique?

A The following table shows some ideas for answering the question above. Check the one that you like the most. If you have your own idea, write it in the last row.

Bird	Feather Characteristics
☐ peacock	• The peacock has very long tail feathers that can grow up to around 1.8 meters long. • The colorful feathers have beautiful eyes on them. The peacock uses its tail feathers to attract females of the species.
☐ macaw	• A macaw is a kind of parrot that has colorful feathers. • Its feathers can be bright red, yellow, or blue, and many of these birds are multicolored, which makes them stand out.
☐ owl	• An owl is able to fly very quietly thanks to its contour feathers. • Its contour feathers are shaped like the teeth of a comb. This reduces the noise while the owl is in flight, so it can hunt prey silently.

B Use one of the ideas in A and write a short paragraph by using the idea.

One bird with interesting feathers is _____. The bird _____.

_____.

The/Its _____

_____.

Unit 12 **Walking Fish**

What is a unique animal that you know about? What characteristics make it unique?

A The following table shows some ideas for answering the question above. Check the one that you like the most. If you have your own idea, write it in the last row.

Animal	Characteristics
☐ okapi	• This animal looks like a combination of a zebra and a giraffe. • It has black and white stripes on its legs and rear that make it look like a zebra. It has a long neck like a giraffe and is also related to the giraffe.
☐ liger	• This animal is the result of a lion and a tiger breeding together. • It may have a mane like a lion and stripes like a tiger. It is also bigger than either a lion or a tiger.
☐ blue dragon	• This animal looks like a tiny version of a dragon. • It lives in the Pacific and Indian oceans. Its blue color helps it blend in with the water. It can deliver a painful sting to people who handle it.

B Use one of the ideas in A and write a short paragraph by using the idea.

One unique animal is _____. This animal _____
_____.
It _____
_____
_____.

Unit 13 Yellow Journalism and Muckraking

Q Do you know a famous reporter or journalist? What did that person do to become famous?

A The following table shows some ideas for answering the question above. Check the one that you like the most. If you have your own idea, write it in the last row.

Reporter/Journalist	Actions
☐ Benjamin Franklin	• This American Founding Father ran a newspaper called the *Pennsylvania Gazette* in the 1730s. • He wrote and printed essays that were known for their humor and satire.
☐ Charles Dickens	• This English novelist worked as a reporter and editor for several newspapers and magazines. • As a reporter, he wrote stories on law and politics, and many of his novels were originally printed in weekly or monthly publications.
☐ Ernest Hemingway	• This American novelist began his writing career as a reporter for the *Kansas City Star*. • He later worked in Canada for the *Toronto Star* and then worked as a foreign correspondent for the newspaper in France.

B Use one of the ideas in A and write a short paragraph by using the idea.

I know about _____ . This _____

_____ .

He/She _____

_____ .

Unit 14 Citizen Journalists

Q What is a news event that citizen journalists helped report on? What happened, and how did the citizen journalists affect news reports?

A The following table shows some ideas for answering the question above. Check the one that you like the most. If you have your own idea, write it in the last row.

News Event	What Happened
☐ 2005 London bombings	• Bombs exploded in London, England. • Citizen journalists took pictures and videos of the places. Many news broadcasters used the pictures and videos for their reports.
☐ 2009 Hudson River plane crash	• A plane crashed in the Hudson River in New York City. • One passenger on a ferry took a photograph of the plane with its passengers getting off it and posted it on Twitter. It became one of the most viewed pictures of the year.
☐ 2004 Boxing Day tsunami	• An earthquake in Southeast Asia created tsunamis that killed hundreds of thousands of people in several countries. • Citizen journalists recorded images of the tsunamis striking shore. They also provided the only pictures and videos of the aftermath of the tsunami for a couple of days.

B Use one of the ideas in A and write a short paragraph by using the idea.

One news event was _____. What happened was that _____

_____.

Then, _____

_____

_____.

Unit 15 **Water in the Solar System**

Q **Where in the solar system do astronomers believe there is water? Why do they feel that water exists there?**

A The following table shows some ideas for answering the question above. Check the one that you like the most. If you have your own idea, write it in the last row.

Location	Reasons
☐ Enceladus	• Astronomers believe this moon of Saturn has a warm, wet, salty ocean. • There are geysers on Enceladus that spew water into outer space. Astronomers think the tidal effects of Saturn give it a liquid ocean.
☐ the moon	• Astronomers think there is ice at the moon's southern pole. • There is also water deep inside the moon. If all of the moon's interior water were liquid, it would form an ocean about one meter deep on the moon's entire surface.
☐ Halley's Comet	• Astronomers know there is ice on this comet that returns to Earth around every seventy-five years. • As Halley's Comet nears the sun, the sun's heat melts some of the ice, which is then expelled in the form of water vapor.

B Use one of the ideas in A and write a short paragraph by using the idea.

One place that may have water is _____. Astronomers _____
_____.

They believe that _____
_____.

Unit 16 Galaxies and Their Formation

Q What is a galaxy that you know about? What type of galaxy is it, and what are its features?

A The following table shows some ideas for answering the question above. Check the one that you like the most. If you have your own idea, write it in the last row.

Galaxy	Type and Features
☐ Andromeda Galaxy	• This is a spiral galaxy and is the closest galaxy to the Milky Way. • It is possible to see the galaxy without using a telescope on a clear, dark night. It is 2.5 million light years away from the Earth.
☐ Bode's Galaxy	• This is a grand spiral galaxy that is found in the constellation called the Big Dipper, or Ursa Major. • It is around 90,000 light years across. It is considered one of the most beautiful galaxies in the night sky.
☐ Porpoise Galaxy	• This is a combination of two galaxies. One is a spiral galaxy while the other is an elliptical galaxy. • It has a unique shape that makes it look like a porpoise. Other people call it the Penguin Galaxy because it looks like a penguin sitting on an egg.

B Use one of the ideas in A and write a short paragraph by using the idea.

I know about (the) _____. This _____
_____.
It _____
_____.

MEMO

Fundamental Reading

PLUS ②